Fifteen

An 826 Valencia Publication

826 Valencia: Tenderloin Center
180 Golden Gate Avenue
San Francisco, CA 94102

826valencia.org

Editor: Molly Parent

Production Manager: Amy Popovich

Design Director: Meghan Ryan

Book Designer: Lucy Kirchner

Cover and Section Illustrations: Dan Bransfield

Production Artist: Patrick Woolf

Copy Editor: Will Georgantas

Printed in Canada by the Prolific Group

Distributed by Publishers Group West

ISBN: 978-1-934750-95-7

Fifteen

BY AUTHORS AGES 8 TO MUCH OLDER THAN 15
FROM 15 YEARS OF 826 VALENCIA

Contents

ZOOM! OFF I GO
FREEDOM, EXCITEMENT, AND THE OPEN ROAD

I THOUGHT I HAD SEEN IT ALL

CHALLENGE, PAINS, AND GAINS

MORE IN COMMON THAN WE MIGHT LIKE TO THINK
ADVICE FOR BEING FIFTEEN AND BEYOND

ABOUT 826 VALENCIA

Foreword

NÍNIVE CALEGARI AND DAVE EGGERS

Dear Community,

We can't thank you enough for all the support, guidance, and heavy lifting you have provided for the last fifteen years. Whether you're an 826 student, volunteer, staff or board member, donor, partner, or just a curious person holding this book because you care about what young people have to say, we thank you for helping this organization evolve and blossom in ways unimaginable when we were young (and we were so young fifteen years ago!).

On the occasion of this milestone birthday, we thought you may enjoy hearing about how the story unfolded—or at least how we remember it.

It all began with a sandwich board on the street. It advertised free tutoring and featured a colorful paper calendar with our schedules and plans on it. This was written in pen. Unlike most marketing today, there was no way to see it or share it unless it was with your own eyes, while walking down the street. We designed a logo to look like our building, put up a website to let folks know about our programs, and started making phone calls to our teacher friends.

Both of us had backgrounds rooted in education—Nínive was a teacher, and Dave had a mother and a sister who were both teachers. We saw a need, we saw the potential for support, and we were eager to help teachers with their own projects and their own ideas. We started 826 Valencia with not much more than this shared vision, a handful of secondhand computers, some desks shaped like worms, and a few core beliefs:

We knew that people were good and generous, and that many of them had spare time.

We knew that young people (and all people) benefit from undivided attention from other caring individuals.

We knew that teachers were working brilliantly at full speed and still needed help, and that even the best teachers don't have enough time to give feedback on writing assignments or undivided attention to every student.

We knew that young people have important stories to tell, and that we needed to create opportunities to share those with a wider audience.

We knew that writing well doesn't require magic or thunderbolts, but rather hard work, revision, and many drafts.

We knew that writing skills and self-expression are vital to finding a path to a happy and fulfilling life.

The first program we offered was After-School Tutoring, an opportunity for students and volunteers to work one-on-one on homework, writing, and publishing, all conveniently located behind San Francisco's only independent Pirate Supply Store. (The space was zoned for retail so we had to sell something, and there was clearly an untapped market there.) We grew our programs by offering workshops on select topics—small classes like This Class Sucks! (on critical writing), cartooning, and journalism. We then built our popular Storytelling & Bookmaking Field Trips, in which classes came to us from all over San Francisco to become published authors in just two hours. Teachers told us that what we were doing was wonderful, and that bringing those resources into the classroom would be even more wonderful. We agreed. So in October of 2002, we pulled a team of ready volunteer tutors and went to Galileo High School to support our first in-school writing project. From there, these core programs grew and blossomed into something bigger and brighter than we'd ever imagined.

As the tutors, parents, and youth started to join us at 826 Valencia Street, we became a constantly humming writing factory, with people of every age working on drafts, manuscripts, editing, and publishing.

Watching young people see professionals at work is immeasurably powerful. Seeing professionals helping younger student authors is clearly powerful. It was a joyful mash-up, and those days were just a small precursor for amazing things to come. 826 chapters started opening in more cities, thanks to more amazing staff and board members, more volunteers, and more glorious students.

This is why today, when we think about the last fifteen years, we just feel excited about the next fifteen, awed by the generosity and beauty of human kindness and human potential.

We want to share a special, humongous shout out to the 826 volunteers who have given time and talent in ways that are too extensive to list. Please know that you taught us that we could do challenging, meaningful, mission-critical work and have a blast at the same time. Your innovation and generosity are beyond measure, and your sense of humor and connection to joy are with us forever.

Finally, we especially thank all the students who shared their truest voices and ideas at 826: your brilliance, your personal and profound resilience, and your hilarious and wonderful work have made every day of this work inspired. Seeing your words as you read them to us from the many 826 books, onstage, in the *New York Times*, at the White House, in *Giants* magazine, and in our everyday lives has been the greatest joy. Thank you for being willing to write another (and another) draft. To those student alums who have gone on to found new chapters of 826 (yes, this happened!), and those who are on staff at 826 now, or teaching, or working with writing in some way, we are so especially proud that you chose to dig in and give back. Happy birthday to you, too. Your ability to thrive is the reason we exist, and we are lucky to have worked with you.

Being Fifteen

MOLLY PARENT

When we, the staff of 826 Valencia, first started to brainstorm ways to celebrate our organization's fifteenth birthday, the room quickly filled with groans and laughter. We were all flooded with memories of that strange and meaningful year of life. Fifteen is when we do a whole lot of growing—physically, emotionally, mentally, and socially—and with that growing comes the clumsiness of adjusting to new ways of being in the world. Sometimes that clumsiness results in formative, perspective-shifting experiences that stay with us for the rest of our lives. Sometimes it just makes for an awkward class photo.

Of course, this makes "being fifteen" a great writing, drawing, or art-making prompt. After all, most stories are about change, and change is what growth is all about. So we rolled up our sleeves and got to work on a book that would capture perspectives on being fifteen from across our community, in all its teenage, transformative glory. We asked our students, volunteers, alumni, friends, and some people who just happened to be walking down the street: What does fifteen mean to you? We also dove into the many student-written publications from the last fifteen years of our programs, which have published thousands of young writers over the years.

As we read through this writing, it became clear that this book is a great example of how a simple prompt—*What does being fifteen mean to you?*—can generate a zillion stories and ideas. As we sifted through the essays, stories, illustrations, poems, and play that make up this book, we were struck by the fact that while there are some universal truths—like the growing pains we all giggled over at the outset of this project—we were actually assembling a testament to the fact that there are as many experiences and associations with being fifteen as there are people in the world (and in this book).

Some of the writers collected here associate being fifteen with the dream car they hope to have someday. *Zoom! Off I go in my car*, writes Calvin, age eleven. Or their plans for the perfect quinceañera. *I will decorate the big room with glow-in-the-dark sticks, balloons, a candy station, and a chocolate fountain. My best friend will be there, and my* tíos *will cook something*, writes Eglys, also age eleven. Some were going through profound changes at age fifteen, handling big decisions that would affect the course of the rest of their lives. *I thought of myself as a grown woman*, writes Gilda, age twenty, *taking care of my younger siblings and the house. My life was already planned; I was going to grow old in the fields similar to all the woman in my town in Guatemala.* Some write about romantic love and heartbreak, some write about friendship, some write about family. All of these experiences of being fifteen are authentic and true.

At 826 Valencia, we believe that writing is a tool for building empathy. That through sharing our stories with the world, we expand our communities and engage with ideas and dreams that might come from a different background than our own. This is a big reason why we do this work, and why we provide free, one-on-one support to help students tell their stories in their own voices with confidence and pride: so that they might influence the thinking of readers they've never met, just as they're influenced and supported by the wider community of caring adults around them.

So, readers of all ages, while hopefully you'll see some of yourself in these pages, we also hope you'll see the stories that are about an entirely different experience of being fifteen than your own. May they make you laugh and cry (two things we associate with being fifteen, and have actually done while editing this collection), and may they perhaps inspire you to put pen to paper to capture whatever time of life you're in, or write a letter to a past or future self, so that your own experiences may be preserved on the page.

And as you read through the remarkable variety of work collected here, you'll notice another theme: hope for the future. So many of the writers and artists collected here are looking forward to what's to come—whether it's the freedom associated with the teenage years that are right around the corner for them, or looking back on their high school selves and whispering "life gets better" through the page. They see their past selves as strong and their future selves as full of possibility. They look ahead, and encourage all of us to do the same. As Blaise, age fifteen, writes: *Water the seeds that have been waiting. . . and let them grow.*

ZOOM!
OFF I GO

FREEDOM, EXCITEMENT, AND THE OPEN ROAD

Learning How to Drive

JASON T.

AGE 11 · LAWTON ALTERNATIVE SCHOOL

Vroom! Vroom! That's the sound of my car's engine. When I'm fifteen, I want to learn how to drive at driving school. I can learn how to drive. I can try to get a driver's license. I can feel what it's like to be in the front seat with so many controls. I would like a beautiful car. I would like a blue and shiny car. I want to hear a smooth, quiet engine. I want to learn how to drive. *Zoom!* Off I go with my car.

Jason enjoys biking and playing on his brother Calvin's laptop in his free time. During the school year, Jason is involved in 826 Valencia's After-School and Evening Tutoring Programs. He has also participated in 826's Exploring Leadership Summer Camp as a youth leader. In the future, he hopes to continue to maintain his good grades.

My First Escape

AUDREY Y.

AGE 16 · PHILLIP & SALA BURTON ACADEMIC HIGH SCHOOL

"Look! The lights just went off!" My friend's nails dug into my arm as she yelled into my ear. It was my first concert. We had been sitting in the plastic seats of Levi's Stadium, waiting for the band to come on. The sky stretched above us, slipping slowly into the evening, and a few lonely stars could be spotted.

Around us, the other concertgoers had been chatting with one another. The smell of cotton candy and popcorn, which were sold by stadium workers, was wafting into the air. But at her words the atmosphere changed.

We sprang up from our seats just as the lights dimmed. The opening played on the screens to the stage and the crowd lit up as phones and cameras began flashing, mirroring the stage. The air was electric as if the stadium as a whole had been struck by lightning. Shouting and laughing filled the air as people jumped up and down in anticipation. Sucked into the atmosphere, all my worries about day-to-day life went away.

"Do you see that?" my friend was still yelling. She had her phone out, poised to capture every moment. As she spoke, the opening notes of the first song began to play. The stadium vibrated with it and the noise escalated. Smoke billowed onto the stage, clouding our vision.

A popping noise sounded in my ears and fireworks exploded into the sky, washing our skin with pinks and oranges. Columns of smoke continued to fill the stage and the band finally emerged. My hands shook where they held my phone. I was rooted to my spot, watching as the screaming reached a breaking point. The band approached the crowd, greeting us. They began their set list. As the night progressed, we grew tired, but the magnetic energy was maintained, practically tangible in the air.

Even though I have had several other concert experiences since then, I will never forget the feelings from the first. I can always look back on it when I want to smile, remembering the excitement and anticipation. My first concert was my first escape, and I will never forget it—from the happiness I felt when my favorite song played, to the laughter my friend and I shared as we recounted our favorite parts on the way home.

Audrey wrote this piece in a Podcasting Field Trip at the 826 Valencia Tenderloin Center. In this program, classes come to our center from all over the city during the school day to write, edit, and record professional podcasts, and learn how to craft an engaging personal story and read it with confidence. Check out 826 Valencia's Message in a Bottle *on SoundCloud to hear more!*

Fifteen Things I Want to Do When I'm Fifteen

ISAAC R.

AGE 10 · CÉSAR CHÁVEZ ELEMENTARY SCHOOL

1. Get a part-time job, like a smoothie or ice cream job.
2. Go to high school.
3. Buy my own food and lunch.
4. Start driving.
5. Buy electronics like a laptop, iPad, and a new iPhone.
6. Have a giant party.
7. Have a car.
8. Take classes to learn new things, like cooking and driving.
9. Buy whatever I want, like in different stores.
10. Do more creative stuff, like drawing or painting.
11. Go to art or drawing classes to get better.
12. Volunteer at places or get another job.
13. Hang out with friends.
14. Go to fun places, like bowling and the arcade.
15. Get good grades.

Isaac has participated in 826 Valencia's Exploring Words Summer Camp. His favorite color is aqua blue. Isaac loves to draw. He has sometimes felt judged because he doesn't play sports, but he won't let that ruin his dreams of becoming an animator when he grows up. He is most inspired by movies (mostly Disney movies).

What's It Like to Be Fifteen?

ANDREA A.

AGE 11 · THOMAS EDISON CHARTER ACADEMY

It will take me four years to be fifteen.

I will be in high school when I am fifteen. The homework will be hard. Something that will be the same is my name and the people I live with. I expect to do better in school when I am fifteen years old. I want to improve my math. I want to get good grades. Right now I am okay at math, I just want to get better. If I study more, I'll get better.

When I'm fifteen, I hope I do more stuff by myself, like cooking lunch, breakfast, and dinner for my family.

When she isn't at school, Andrea enjoys spending her free time reading and drawing. When she grows up, she wants to be a dentist or a doctor. She is involved with 826 Valencia's After-School Tutoring Program and Exploring Leadership Summer Camp.

The Big Day

GABRIELA T.

AGE 11 · HERBERT HOOVER MIDDLE SCHOOL

It was the big day: I was finally turning fifteen. I felt excited, happy, nervous; I felt a lot of emotions. At that same moment, I wondered what would change and what would stay the same. Would I move or would I live in the same house? I had a lot of questions of how it would go for me.

My biggest goal was to get good grades at school so I could be ready for college. I wondered how my life would be being fifteen.

As I went down the stairs, the smell of my favorite foods filled the air, but I didn't hear anything or anyone as I took the last step. SURPRISE! It was a surprise party!

Everybody celebrated with me for my fifteenth birthday.

Gabriela wrote this piece in the 2017 Exploring Leadership Summer Camp at 826 Valencia, where she spent her summer building leadership skills and serving as a tutor and mentor to elementary school students.

Imaginary Ocean

ALICE MALIA

In 1997 when I was fifteen, I painted the whole of my friend's bathroom with an epic underwater theme! Perhaps I hoped it would bring me closer to being a mermaid. Today I am an illustrator and theater set designer. I am originally from the UK; now I live in San Francisco with my husband and my toddler. I love living close to the sea, I am still no closer to being a mermaid, but I keep drawing and painting and hoping.

Alice Malia has been involved with 826 Valencia as a volunteer illustrator for two years, painting everything from a treehouse full of students for our annual appeal, to a banana-loving cat-dog for the 826 Quarterly *anthology.*

ART: Alice Malia

The Great Debate

JESUS R.

AGE 10 · BUENA VISTA HORACE MANN K-8

I had just turned fifteen. It was 2022 and it was soccer season. It was a good day to play soccer, but Donald Trump wanted to turn the soccer stadium into a golf course.

I did not play soccer as much as I played when I was little. Now I had to work at a pool as a lifeguard. One day I had a day off and I wanted to play soccer, but the soccer stadium was not there. It was a golf course. So, I thought, *who likes to play golf?* I thought of Donald Trump and I knew it was him, so I looked for him.

Then I found him and I asked him, "Why did you turn the soccer stadium into a golf course? Please turn it back into a soccer stadium."

But he said, "No."

I said I'd debate him for it. The date of the debate came. I was nervous, but I knew I was going to win. I was only fifteen, but I'd known that soccer stadium for years.

All the people who played soccer on the field voted for me. The votes were counted, and I was down 400 to 450. Then I put a TV up and showed them memories of the soccer stadium. The final score was 501 to 499. I won, but I knew I couldn't have done this without the help of my friends and family.

Jesus has worked with 826 Valencia at Exploring Words Summer Camp and in the after-school program at Buena Vista Horace Mann K–8. He works hard at 826 because he wants to make his tutors happy. His favorite activity is playing soccer on the Jamestown soccer team.

When I'm Fifteen

JOANNA H.

AGE 13 · ROOSEVELT MIDDLE SCHOOL

When I'm fifteen I want to help my mom and dad make a living. When I'm fifteen, I will be in high school; Washington, I hope. When I'm fifteen I will have a fifteenth birthday just like my cousin and my sister did. When I'm fifteen, I will get better at soccer and basketball. When I'm fifteen, I will be able to make more food than I know how to make now. When I'm fifteen I will be taller. When I'm fifteen, I will try new things. When I'm fifteen, I will find out what I want to be in life.

Joanna likes to play sports and be with friends. In the future she wants to go to UC Berkeley and become a lawyer, because she likes to argue with people. She is involved in 826 Valencia's After-School Tutoring Program and Exploring Leadership Summer Camp.

Going to Mexico and Hawaii

JESSICA P.

AGE 10 · BUENA VISTA HORACE MANN K-8

When I'm fifteen, I really want to go to Mexico. I want to put flowers on my grandpa's grave because my grandpa died and I want to go visit his grave. I hope I can do this because I miss him so much. At least he's in heaven for me.

Also, Mexico is my country! I also want to go there because I want to explore the towns and go hiking. Some people there sew blankets and almost everything else and sell them. It's so colorful in Mexico.

I really want to go to Hawaii because the water is so clean and so clear that you can open your eyes underwater. You don't have to bring goggles to Hawaii, and that's so cool. There is this place where you can swim with the dolphins. There are also stores that sell cool and awesome stuff like necklaces with shark teeth and pretty earrings.

Jessica's favorite hobby is swimming in the pool, because swimming is fun even without dolphins around. She has worked with 826 Valencia in the after-school program at Buena Vista Horace Mann K–8 and in Exploring Words Summer Camp.

What Will Happen When I Turn Fifteen

DOMINIC C.

AGE 10 · CÉSAR CHÁVEZ ELEMENTARY SCHOOL

When I turn fifteen, I do not want to be lazy. I will always do my work and I do not want to fail and I want to get a job. I want to get my driver's license and go to college. I want to play basketball on the high school team and I want to be the point guard. I want my jersey number to be 29. I want to do good so I can graduate.

Dominic worked with 826 Valencia in the third grade and again in Exploring Words Summer Camp. He likes to play basketball, and wants to be an NBA player when he grows up.

A One-Man Army

JAVIER L.

AGE 15 · SAN FRANCISCO INTERNATIONAL HIGH SCHOOL

"**Hey Javier, you** are a one-man army," my teacher said. That was me, sitting by myself at a computer coding a game at Mission Bit, an after-school program for coding. During the program, we had a final project for a competition to build whatever our team wanted. In my group of four, two people decided not to show up anymore without saying anything. My other teammate and I felt doomed, like a mechanic without his tools.

Quitting was not one of our options. In this tough situation, our goal was to learn and gain experience and exposure in this program. Because two of our members left, we made a plan for a simple game that we knew we could finish on time. We used our resources as much as possible, and we weren't afraid to ask for help.

One day I made a lot progress in my game and tried to save it on the computer at the end of the day. But by accident, I erased everything I did during that day. I felt angry and I thought, *Why did this happen to me?* The things I learned that day helped me gain momentum, and I didn't have any reasons to give up. So I continued working and redid everything that I did that day and made it even better.

Three weeks later, we were at the competition with groups from different schools. There were about ten teams in total. My teammate and I thought that we had zero chance to win against the other teams. However, we were satisfied to at least try and have a final product. So we were sitting in the back watching the other awards being given. Suddenly, the announcer said, "In second place, Javier and Rachel for their game, Reach for the Sky!"

I said, "What? Are you kidding me right now?" And we looked at each other with confusion and surprise.

We went up to the stage to get our award and I couldn't stop smiling for the rest of the day. My teacher was really proud of me and said, "Wow, the one-man army really worked out."

This experience was really important to me because I always look back to it every time I have hard times in my life. Even when a challenge is not on a computer, I learned that I can work hard and do my best and that I am capable of overcoming problems. I couldn't quit but I am glad that I stuck with it. I know now that I can achieve my goals by working hard. This amazing experience made me more interested in programming and consider it for my future.

Javier wrote this piece in a Podcasting Field trip at the 826 Valencia Tenderloin Center. In this program, classes come to our center from all over the city during the school day to write, edit, and record professional podcasts, and learn how to craft an engaging personal story and read it with confidence. Check out 826 Valencia's Message in a Bottle *on SoundCloud to hear more!*

Plans for My Fifteenth Party

GISSETLE A.

AGE 10 · CÉSAR CHÁVEZ ELEMENTARY SCHOOL

I am excited for my fifteenth year. My dress will be light aqua. There will be a big screen showing pictures and videos of when I was little. I was so cute. My mom and my best friend are going to help with my dress and my makeup. I will have long, fake eyelashes. I'm going to have red lipstick and high heels that match my dress. There will be a big cake and ice cream. I will come in a limo and everybody will be waiting for me. My limo will have a big bow with flowers. When I walk, I will be holding a bouquet of flowers. There will be a red carpet. As I walk, they will throw flowers. There will be a big chocolate fountain. There's going to be a big table of treats. Chefs will be passing food out. There will be someone playing the piano and someone playing the violin and someone playing the cello. When I feel like it, I can play the violin. My quinceañera party is going to be big.

Gissetle plans to be a famous actor and star in movies when she grows up. She has visited 826 Valencia on Field Trips with her school and participated in Exploring Words Summer Camp. She appreciates her tutor, Dana, for helping her.

How I Hope Fifteen Will Be

CALVIN T.

AGE 14 · BALBOA HIGH SCHOOL

My name is Calvin and I am fourteen years old. Fifteen is just next year for me and there isn't a lot to look forward to.

When I'm fifteen I really want to get a driver's license so when I turn sixteen, I can immediately start driving. I will turn sixteen at the end of the tenth grade. That means the summer between tenth and eleventh grade, I will start driving around.

It would be really nice to get a new car. Something like a McLaren MP4-12C. It costs around $180,000, so I have high doubts I can get it. If I do get it, I can imagine the amazing sound of the engine. It would be an extremely smooth ride because of the dual-clutch transmission. It has also been a while since I smelled a new-car smell, so that would be nice, too. I'm probably going to drive to school every day. I can imagine myself getting a speeding ticket about every week.

When I'm fifteen I also want a way to make money, but who knows how that will happen.

When he isn't at school, Calvin enjoys playing games on his computer. He hopes to get a very high-paying job in the future to buy nice cars, a house, and to help his family. Calvin has been involved in 826 Valencia's After-School Tutoring Program, Workshops, Youth Leadership Advisory Board, and Exploring Leadership Summer Camp.

Self Portrait

MEI HSUAN CHIANG

This image was created to show a teenage girl who always likes to spend her summertime at the beach, where she can be alone and be creative. Growing plants represent her thoughts.

Mei Hsaun Chiang is a professional illustrator based in San Francisco and Taipei. She likes to paint, read, and sip a cup of coffee every day. She first got involved with 826 Valencia as a volunteer illustrator during the summer of 2016, creating art for the Exploring Words Summer Camp chapbook titled This Is the Wild. *You can view her work at* meihsuanchiang.com.

ART: **Mei Hsuan Chiang**

My Fifteenth Dream

KIARA F.

AGE 9 · BUENA VISTA HORACE MANN K-8

When I'm fifteen, I want to have either a pet gorilla or a cheetah. The cheetah's name will be Micaila and the gorilla, Skylar.

I want to live in a mansion with a big gigantic pool. The gorilla will eat bananas. The cheetah will eat steak and chicken. I would want to train them to protect me, so if any people try to break in they will protect me. I would also want to train them to let me ride on their backs.

I would want a big jeep to fit my gorilla and cheetah. And the jeep will be blue.

My mansion will be covered in blue slime. There will be a room with slime. My room will only have a little slime. And the color of my room will be aqua blue.

And in the backyard, I will have a race in the pool with my pets. And that's my ending!

Kiara worked with 826 Valencia during Exploring Words Summer Camp. She loves animals and has a pit bull named Savvy. She would like to dedicate this piece to her tutor, Dana.

How It Will Feel to Be Fifteen

EDUARDO G.

AGE 11 · THOMAS EDISON CHARTER ACADEMY

I am four to five and a half years away from being fifteen. When I'm fifteen, I want to be better in high school. I will be excited for math classes because math is challenging, but you can also learn more from being challenged.

I want $1,000 so I can save for my dream car. My dream car is a fast, cool Lamborghini. Getting this car will be a challenge because it will cost around $35,900,000. And if I could afford it, I could get a Nissan GTR that will cost around $45,500.

I can't wait to be fifteen!

In his free time, Eduardo enjoys playing games on his phone, like Clash Royale. *Eduardo loves cars, and in the future he wants to be a mechanic. Eduardo has been involved in 826 Valencia's After-School Tutoring Program and Exploring Leadership Summer Camp.*

My Fifteen-Years Party Dreams

EGLYS A.

AGE 11 · CÉSAR CHÁVEZ ELEMENTARY SCHOOL

I want my dress to be red. I also want my quinceañera in a really big room. I will have all my friends and my family there. I will have a big *tres leches* cake and on top will be a Barbie because when I was little I liked Barbie.

Something I really want to do is have a dance with my dad, because that is traditional for Latinos. I will have a red limo and use it to go places with my friends and dance.

I will decorate the big room with glow-in-the-dark sticks, balloons, a candy station, and a chocolate fountain. My best friend will be there, and my *tíos* will cook something. I will be so happy about my quinceañera.

Eglys dreams of being a famous singer when she grows up. She has visited 826 Valencia with her class on field trips and participated in Exploring Words Summer Camp.

The Real Me!

LANIYA B.

AGE 15 · SUMMER BRIDGE

They call me the funny girl.
The girl who brings laughter to the whole world.
The hype and the voice to the real world.
They call me Lion because I'm the voice of the roar.
The talent they see in me is the dream they're soon to see.
I'm R&B and '80s, a little old-school, even though
I'm just fifteen.
I ain't shy because I'm free.
I ain't scared because I'm free.
I'm living in the world
where my life belongs to no one but me.

Laniya wrote this piece during the first summer of program partnerships at the 826 Valencia Tenderloin Center. 826 Valencia tutors supported students from Summer Bridge and other summer enrichment programs as they worked on a variety of writing projects.

The Striped Blue Afghan

ERICA LORRAINE SCHEIDT

The striped blue afghan is already on his lap and I pull it on mine. It's late and my sister is out with his sister and we're watching *Twilight Zone*, the movie, in his parents' den and his hand reaches out and holds my hand under the afghan. I can't speak. My face is hot and I feel the whole hot world in the flesh of his hand. I'm already telling myself the story of how my sister was out with his sister and how we watched *Twilight Zone*, the movie, and he held my hand. And that tight ache in my stomach and sting on my lips that I keep licking means that we're going to kiss. We are going to kiss. I clutch at his hand. I slump down low even though it's dark in the room with just the light of the television. He hunches down too and we're under the afghan that smells like corn chips and yarn. We hold hands and hunch down so that our faces are under the afghan and moving, nuzzling toward each other. I know he must have kissed before. He's older. And his lips are soft. And then I'm telling myself the story of how he kissed me. And kiss and kiss and kiss like babies, breathing into each other's mouths. We kiss for minutes and hours and after *Twilight Zone*, the movie. And through the news. And the story about the missing hiker. And the weather. Still with one sweaty hand clutching another.

Erica Lorraine Scheidt is the author of the young adult novel Uses for Boys. *She volunteered at 826 Valencia for more than nine years before figuring out that she wanted to be a public school teacher. She now teaches high school in Oakland, California.*

Well, There Was No Tongue Dancing

MARIA R.

AGE 16 · IMMACULATE CONCEPTION ACADEMY

The message was clear when my eyes met his. It was happening. Today. It seemed like such an established event, I felt it was almost appropriate to put it on my calendar with a date, time, and location.

I hadn't seen him since our eighth-grade graduation. A short boy with a mop of curly, black hair awkwardly placed on his head, the most vivid memory I had of him was when we were in the sixth grade. We were on our outdoor education trip and, for no reason at all, he rammed me into the small creek we were exploring. Now here he was, five years later, participating in the same web design internship I was so hesitant to apply to. I almost didn't recognize him the first day we were in the office together. He looked different, taller, with sharper facial features. Puberty had been good to him, I thought. He definitely had better manners. But what surprised me the most was that out of all the people I wanted to lay one on me, he made his way from being one of the last to one of the first.

I stole glances at him from behind the gigantic screen of my monitor, careful not to make eye contact a second time. That would look needy. But at the same time, all I wanted to do was look into those gorgeous brown eyes—like God had made his irises out of honey and added in small flecks of gold. He had those cute lips, the kind that male models often have to have photoshopped on their faces, the kind most girls consider "kissable," the kind I'm going to. . .

I was pulled out of my girlish daydream by a sharp chime coming from the main monitor. Five thirty. Oh God, this is it. This is real life.

It's happening. I quickly packed up my things, making sure I wasn't leaving anything behind because there would be no time to come back.

I silently slipped away from the office and half walking, half running, made my way to the farthest staircase, the only one that had a small platform with a single window that gave a peeking view of the neighboring building's roof garden. And then I just stood there. Waiting. Anticipating. Worrying. What if I'm a horrible kisser? What do I do with my hands? Oh God, what if my hair gets in his mouth? Maybe I should put my hair in a ponytail. But ponytails aren't sexy. Yeah, no, that's a no-go on the ponytail.

I stood there for what seemed like hours, palms sweaty, heart pounding. Pounding way too fast, actually. I was almost sure my heart was thudding the number of beats per minute that indicates when a person is about to go into cardiac arrest. Come on, where was he? I checked my phone. 5:34 p.m.

"It's only been four minutes," I growled at myself, "Get a grip."

I waited another two. Maybe I had gotten the wrong message. Maybe this wasn't going to happen today. Maybe this wasn't going to happen at all. It could have been that he'd just glanced at me. I mean, we were friends. What if I'd just made a complete fool of myself?

I heard the gentle *pah-dha*, *pah-dha* of his sneakers getting progressively louder as he walked from the hallway into the corridor of the staircase. He smiled, those supermodel lips curving up, creating small dimples. He came up to me, totally confident, and just stared directly into my eyes. In that moment, I could have sworn that the walls just melted away. There was absolutely no sound and the world was spinning. He opened his mouth as if to ask me a question, closed it, slightly parted his lips again, and leaned in. That's my cue, I thought, and we closed our eyes, those beautiful brown eyes disappearing in a black cloak of darkness.

His lips lightly leafed against mine, like two pieces of crisp paper trying not to crinkle. His mouth was dry and he kept twisting his head in such an exaggerated left-and-right motion I was scared his neck was going to break. Instead of meshing, our lips were pulling at the ends and chafing painfully. I thought maybe I was just leaning too far back, so I tried to lean forward, and as I did his teeth kept clashing with mine as if they were the locked gates of a golden city I was forbidden to enter. Maybe this kiss was like a concert: You have to get through the opening act before you can enjoy the main event. So I waited, trying to mend the broken rhythm of our bodies with my arms around his neck, his arms by his sides. And then it finally hit me: This was the main event. This is what I had waited in line for—a sold-out show where we find that the only performer sounds better on a CD than he does live. As quickly as it had started, it was over. He stopped and I opened my eyes to see him smirking back at me.

"I hope that makes up for the shove in the river. See you around."

With a quick wink, he walked away with the strut of a champion.

Um, wait, what? That was it? That was the big kiss that I had been anticipating since watching *Titanic*? Was this a joke? Please tell me this was a joke. Nope, he was gone. That was really it. Was that satisfying for him? Did he really believe that I was going to be impressed by the awkward clamoring of teeth or that horrible feeling of dry lips scraping against my own? Walking away, he gave the impression that he'd just given me the best possible first kiss a human being could possibly give to another. I felt a little embarrassed for him, that he could be so painfully wrong.

Some books give you all this descriptive detail about magical kisses: Their tongues danced, his lips crashed onto hers, she heard fireworks going off in her head. All these beautiful, passionate scenes of these kisses that somehow have become this stereotypical and symbolic rite of passage into womanhood. Well, there was no tongue dancing. I don't know how there were going to be crashing lips if there were hardly any lips to begin with. Like, they were only on his face for the purpose of decoration. There most definitely weren't any sparks. I felt like I was burning in a forest fire when I was waiting by myself, in the moment leading up to the kiss. The kiss, if you can even call it one, was like a rainstorm that completely extinguished every single flame, not even leaving a tiny little ember that survived.

Maria wrote this essay in the 2014 Young Authors' Workshop at 826 Valencia. Her reading of it at the end of the program brought the house down, and led to her being invited to revise and perform the piece for Radio Ambulante's *bilingual live show that fall. Maria was the show's only teen storyteller—and she received a standing ovation! She now attends San Francisco State University.*

I THOUGHT I HAD SEEN IT ALL

CHALLENGE, PAINS, AND GAINS

How I Thought of Myself at Fifteen Years Old

GILDA TEMAJ MARROQUIN

AGE 20 · SAN FRANCISCO INTERNATIONAL HIGH SCHOOL

When I was fifteen years old I thought I had seen it all. I thought of myself as a grown woman—taking care of my younger siblings and the house. My life was already planned; I was going to grow old in the fields similar to all the women in my town in Guatemala. I could not think of something different because there was not such a thing. I knew I was living the life I was supposed to live, but I still felt incomplete. I knew I was missing something.

One day after the meal at noon, all my family left to continue the work in the fields, and I stared outside the window to look far in the horizon where everything seemed peaceful. Standing there, I would ask myself questions like, *Gilda, are you happy? What would happen if you left?*

I had spent six years asking myself the same questions when I decided to leave. Sitting around my sisters and my mom, I shared my goals with them. I told them that I wanted to have a house and be independent, therefore I decided to immigrate to the United States. With distress in her eyes my mom looked at me, feeling guilty for giving me false hopes. She just nodded her head in agreement before sending me back to do my chores. I imagine she was feeling sorry for me because at fifteen, I was dreaming of accomplishing many things in a place where the reality was different.

But I am glad that my dreams persisted and did not vanish like the dreams of most people in my town. Feeling empowered and determined with a heart full of dreams, I left Guatemala at sixteen without looking behind.

It's been five years since I was fifteen, and because of the desire, initiative, and determination of that fifteen-year-old girl I have built myself a better future. I have graduated from San Francisco International High School, and in the fall I will be attending UC Berkeley. I thought I knew about what to expect from life when I was fifteen, but now my future life is full of new and different opportunities. If I were fifteen again I would do exactly what I did: find my own path.

Gilda Temaj Marroquin, a 2017 826 Valencia Scholarship Winner, graduated from San Francisco International High School and is now a freshman at UC Berkeley. Since moving to the United States she has become an advocate for girls' education, starting with her younger sisters. Whether exploring civil rights with the ACLU or conducting biomedical research with UCSF, she continues to challenge herself and explore uncharted territories.

Pink Fingernails and Foreign Affairs

IRIS M.

AGE 14 · NUEVA SCHOOL

Being a teenage girl influences my life and perception in a way unlike that of any other identity. Unlike other demographics, teenage girls are stereotyped in a way such that all of my interests are deemed inferior and "typical," or otherwise so outlandishly peculiar for someone of my age and gender that I mustn't really understand them. Think about what is marketed to female adolescents—cosmetics, boy bands, true love, and the color pink—and consider the fact that these things are so excessively insistent upon my investment that it is nearly impossible to avoid them. People seem to have an outlook—one that bleeds into their interactions—that insists that teenage girls' opinions are not relevant, that they are autonomous at times but influenced by popular media, and above all, that the things we like or are supposed to like are objectively inferior. Any variation of these opinions promotes the idea that all of the opinions, abilities, and business impacts that we possess are not to be taken seriously, and because of this, my peers and I all suffer. I do like things that I am told to, and though I can acknowledge that they are not entirely autonomous opinions, I am still entitled to them, and wish so much that people would respect my opinions without judgment.

I want to exist as more than my label as a teenage girl, or rather, I want expectations and opinions of me to be structured independently. I want to be able to flip the pages of *Foreign Affairs* with pink fingernails. I want to read James Joyce and John Green and to not contradict myself. And furthermore, I want nothing I do to contradict my status, nothing I like to be compared to what I'm supposed to. We are living in a world where the same people who market to us feminine things accuse us of being idiotic for liking them—and I cannot change this. I cannot stop being a teenage girl.

Being a teenage girl is a unique position, as my social role and interpretation is different from those of women of any other age group. An adult woman practically has a list of prescribed responsibilities, and while these are not as interesting or impactful as those of a man, they still exist. Teenage girls, on the other hand, are often considered useless, aside from the money they spend and their status as subordinates to their male counterparts (cheerleaders, if you will). "Grown-ups," or older people in general, use their power to control what we like via PR firms and ads in teen girl magazines to encourage us to purchase things, and in the same breath can accuse us of being idiotic for wanting them. As writers before me have suggested (see: Hazel Cills and others), perhaps this is the case because the people in these positions of power—too often men and too rarely minorities—have been told for a very long time that their opinions are the *right* ones, and, however subconsciously, they are discouraged from considering others. These people are often taught to believe that teenage-girlish things are bad, and this opinion leads them to be bigoted in their treatment of feminine adolescents. In any event, these associations against teenage girls manifest the fact that women can have different roles in our society—adults are wives and mothers and secretaries, while teenage girls are cheerleaders and an easy consumer demographic.

Though anyone might find adolescence upsetting, heightened misogyny makes teenage girlhood uniquely unfavorable. Adolescence is synonymous with many unpleasant things, like hyperactive sexuality, acne, and raging hormones, but our society also enforces gender-based principles that make being a teenage girl a very different experience from being a teenage boy. In our society, men and women have assigned colors, haircuts, and a whole host of other associations, but for teenagers, these things are often more definitively negative or positive. For example, teenage boys are encouraged or sometimes expected to partake in sports, whereas a teenage girl might be expected to go shopping for cosmetics and clothing. You can ask the average person which they think is more productive or interesting, and they will almost definitely tell you that sports are better, somehow, than shopping. Perhaps they are, but that shouldn't mean that teenage boys are better than teenage girls, no? Interestingly, this is also often the case for negative associations with boys—vandalism, light violence, and other characteristically bad things associated with boys are far too often thought of with a "boys will be boys" attitude. Even when they do things that in no way are helpful or contributive, their actions are often seen in a positive light.

Sometimes, the opposite is true for teenage girls—no matter what we do, even if it conforms to expectations, someone will always insist that we are doing things wrong. If we *don't* align ourselves with these feminine interests, activities, and behaviors, someone will always tell us that we need to revert to our assigned roles in society. "Wouldn't the best thing now be to let her focus on her GCSEs and A-levels?" asks Rob Crilly, in a blog post for the *Telegraph* about Malala Yousafzai. "Don't get me wrong," he continues. "It would be a remarkable story were she to win the Nobel Peace Prize. . . But at what price to a teenage girl? I for one will be quietly hoping she doesn't win."

No matter what we understand or choose to engage in, individuals with greater perceived cultural influence will always judge us negatively. Furthermore, I would like to suggest that this idea is cyclical in nature. Constantly, our society is generating media about teenage girls that increase negative associations. These articles have a certain familiarity to them. As popular singer/teenage girl activist Lorde said in an interview, "There's a definite viewpoint of the think piece by an adult writing about kids." As Lorde and her famous teenage cohort know better than anybody, articles like this do little more than reinforce societal associations with youth and femininity, and these associations go on to greatly impact the way we live our lives. As a recent study published in the *New York Times* by Seth Stephens-Davidowitz and many others like it show, parents have great bias in their opinion of their child based on gender. In this case, parents are 250 percent more likely to Google-search whether or not their son is gifted than their daughter. It's a cycle; media creators reinforce gender roles, media recipients act based upon them. The victims of these harmful associations, teenage girls, have little power to change it.

Despite all of this, my feminine adolescence is inevitable, and like you and all grown-ups and everyone else, I somehow coveted it throughout my childhood. As a younger child, I was infatuated with the idea of being a teenager. I'm sure that this, too, stemmed in part from media portrayal, but I also believe that to a certain extent, it is innate. I recall wistfully the times as a young child when I would bond with friends over our teenager escapades, giving ourselves new names and habits just so that we could try to escape the tyranny of youth. On occasion, I remember lightly lying about how old I was, perhaps because I didn't *feel* eight or nine years old, but also because I wanted nothing more than for these statements to be true. Honestly, I could still lie about my age, and though I mightn't convince anybody, I could still try. If I truly believed that it would be better to be twenty or eighteen or anything but my fourteen-year-old self, I could escape to the Internet where I have no real identity and create a new self entirely. Doing this might make people more inclined to listen to my opinions, something that frustrates me to no end, but given that it is inevitable in reality that I will be labeled, categorized, and stereotyped as a teenage girl, I see pride as truly my best option. If I can, to any extent, convince people that teenage girls have something to offer the world, I can—we can—change the dynamic.

Iris wrote and revised this essay in the Writing and Publishing Apprentices workshop at 826 Valencia in 2014. It was published in the chapbook Songs and Robots and Home and Us, *and in* the 826 Quarterly, *vol. 21.*

When I Was Fifteen

MATTHEW ZAPRUDER

When I was fifteen
I suddenly knew
I would never
understand geometry.
Who was my teacher?
That name is gone.
I only remember
the gray feeling
in a classroom
filled with vast
theoretical distances.
I can still see
odd shapes
drawn on the board,
and those inscrutable
formulas everyone
was busily into
their notebooks scribbling.
I looked down
at the Velcro
straps of my entirely
white shoes and knew
inside me things
had long ago gone
terribly wrong
and would continue
for a long time

to be. When
the field hockey star
broke her knee,
I wrote a story
for the school paper
then brought her
the history notes
in the snow.
She stood
in the threshold,
a whole fire-lit life
of mysterious
familial warmth
glowing behind her,
and took them
from my hands
like the blameless
queen of elegant
violence she was.
Walking home
encased in immense
amounts of down
I listened to
the analog ghost
in the machine
pour from the cassette
I had drawn
flowers on.
Into my ears
it sang everything
they told you
makes you believe
you are trapped
in a snow globe
forgotten in a dark
closet where exhausted
shadows argue
what is sorrow

cannot become joy,
but I am here
from the future
to tell you
you are not,
all you must do
is stay asleep
a few more years
great traveler waiting to go.

Matthew Zapruder is the author of four books of poetry and Why Poetry, *a book of prose about poetry, available from Ecco/HarperCollins in August 2017. An associate professor in the MFA program at Saint Mary's College of California, he is also editor at large at Wave Books. He lives in Oakland. A longtime friend and admirer of 826 Valencia, he has guest-taught many creative writing classes and written an introduction, "Little Surrealists,"* for *the 826 Quarterly.*

Fifteen Going On. . .

TIM R.

Fifteen is and was an odd tangle of time. Your skin is supple and young, but also fleshy and oily. It's just starting to find its contours. You start to know things, even understand them enough to fight what you think they mean. Feelings. Ugh, feelings especially.

And everything is new. Every day is discovering America, and you want everyone to know it—even if you don't want them staring at you. But America is hard to settle if you've just moved to Tokyo because your parents want you to be "closer to home." Even though home has always been a preppy suburb in L.A., not some congested, flashing urban progress of trains and towers halfway around the world.

I'd had no plans of moving anywhere—not at fifteen, and not with my mom, just us. But maybe that's the perfect storm a fifteen-year-old needs. Having to figure out which train to catch the transfer for school, or which milk carton design means low fat when you can't read a word, is complicated and frustrating. Looking back, that's a good thing. Having a bigger worldview forced onto you is great yeast for who you can eventually be.

Eventually you grow up—sort of. You're always "the kid" until you turn 28. But time still only goes in one direction in our neck of the galaxy. Tangles and knots pull apart or tighten, and the exercise of being fifteen does the same. The only thing we can do is decide whether to give ourselves some slack, or impatiently pick at the things that can't be untied.

Tim is a design volunteer, Pirate Store clerk, and all-around helper at 826 Valencia. He came to San Francisco's Mission District for the sunshine, but has discovered so much more to love: free yoga, homemade bikes, mandated composting and recycling, cheap Mexican food, the J MUNI line, and 826. You can see his work at subject-object.net.

ART: **Cristina Lalli**

Escape Plan

CRISTINA LALLI

Fifteen isn't an easy age for most, and it was no exception for me. Things were changing, and my increasingly cynical teenage mind was not amused. All I could think of was how and when I would escape, whatever that meant. I imagined it had something to do with a car, Björk, and college. I participated in as many high school extracurriculars as possible, like field hockey, school newspaper, art explorers club, all the while writing, drawing, and dreaming about my method of escaping high school. Being a teenager in the suburbs of Ohio meant being literally stuck in one place without access to an automobile. There was no subway, underground, or L train. The bus was barely an option. Every teenager I knew had the same obsession: getting your "temps." The ultimate irony being that an adult, licensed driver was legally obligated to accompany you. It would just have to wait, at least another year.

I've since managed to "escape," and no longer own a car.

Cristina Lalli is a former graphic designer and classroom teacher turned children's book illustrator, currently living in London. She has taught in special needs public school classrooms in both New York City and London, but it was 826CHI in Chicago where she cut her teeth with after-school homework help, in-school trips, field trips, and creative workshops. It was during this time she knew for certain that she wanted a future in children's literacy, whether it be in the form of teaching, writing, drawing, or making books.

Young African American Problems

JAMES J.

AGE 15 · JOHN O'CONNELL HIGH SCHOOL

I **am a** fifteen-year-old African American male who gets misjudged for a lot of racial things. Because of my ethnicity, there's a lot of clothing and hairstyles I can't wear, and groups I can't be with. I know you guys are probably saying, "Doesn't everybody have things like that?" No! Is that right or fair that I get treated the way I do? No, it isn't right or fair, so I would like to speak up about it.

I had my first experience with racial stereotyping when I was thirteen years old. I was wearing a black hoodie tied so that you really couldn't see my face, with black Levi's jeans and black Jordans. My pants were down kind of low, but I was still walking pretty fast. And it just so happened, at that time, a crime had been committed and I fit the description of the criminal. However, I was shorter than the person who had committed the crime. All of a sudden, three police cars came speeding up with their sirens on and lights flashing. Three officers were standing behind their car doors slightly crouching with their guns pointing at me like I was dangerous.

The officer yelled, "Put your hands in the air and get down slowly!" With a terrified face I did what was asked of me without any weird or sudden moves. *Click click click click click*, the sound the shoes made as the cops ran toward me. Then, *boom!* the sound my body made, hitting the hard, cold concrete. *Zip zip* is what I heard as I felt hard, cold metal being put on my wrists. They picked me up and began reading me my rights as a large crowd looked at me with disgust. Two hours after arriving at juvenile hall, I was released and apologized to for the way I had been treated, and for being brought in for nothing.

There's not a day that goes by without me remembering that incident, and so I make sure I'm dressed well and don't look like a criminal. While out in public, I don't like to be with the type of people who talk way too loudly and act like they have no sense. Once my friends and I were walking home from school and there was this white boy in front of us by himself. He was about four feet, ten inches tall, and weighed about 120 pounds; he had dirty blond hair and blue eyes. Then there were my friends: tall, loud, and reckless. These are the type of people who would wear black sweaters in 110-degree weather talking about things they have recently stolen. The boy in front of us started to get worried and scared. I started to notice his actions more because he kept looking over his shoulder with a worried look on his face. Even though he's my neighbor, he seemed not to recognize me; yet we talk every day. I began to call for him. "Jake, Jake, Jake!" I yelled, trying to get his attention. It wasn't working, so I started jogging toward him, continuing to call for him. The group followed right behind.

Then it happened. "Leave me alone! Stop following me!" he screamed, and took off in a sprint while on the phone with the police. We stopped jogging and stood there, startled about what he had just said, and we sat there and just thought to ourselves. Five minutes later, when we finally arrived at my house, he was outside talking to the police and was pointing at us as we grew closer. The police officer asked us what happened and we explained. Jake felt bad about what had happened and made up for it later in life. He and his family took me with them on a family vacation to Lake Tahoe during winter.

I try not to be out past nine o'clock. That's when the police and criminals are out. That's also when people can become very rude. For example, there are times when I have walked down streets and heard, *chirp-chirp, chirp-chirp ,chirp-chirp, chirp-chirp*, the sound of people setting their car alarms four times to make sure it's locked. Or other times, when families would just stand by their car and wait until I am far away from them before entering their house. People may not notice, but I see how I am treated differently because of my race, which is totally unjustified.

In today's world, African Americans get treated the worst compared to other races. It feels like it's ten times harder for us to get a job than for a white person. Or if I walk into a store, I get watched closely because they think I might steal something. The color of my skin doesn't determine my characteristics or my actions. I believe in equal chances and fairness. So, do I think stereotypes are fair? No, I don't. I really think people should get to know a person before making assumptions. As Malcolm X once said, "I believe in human beings, and that all human beings should be respected as such, regardless of their color."

James wrote this essay as part of the 2013 Me to We project at John O'Connell High School. In this project, students worked with 826 Valencia tutors to write autobiographical narratives about a group they belong to, with the goal of increasing understanding across different backgrounds. This piece was first published in the chapbook Creatures in the Fog *and in* the 826 Quarterly, *vol. 19.*

Teenage Poetry

KATE SCHATZ

I have been writing for as long as I can remember, but my first memory of writing something that felt "grown up" (as in: Complex! Intellectual! Not just *Babysitters Club* fan fiction!) comes from 1994, when I was freshly fifteen and sat cross-legged on the floor of my bedroom, door locked (my parents had caved and let me have a lock!), likely listening to Led Zeppelin. There, in a burst of inspiration, I wrote some Poetry (capital *P* on purpose). Three Poems, to be exact, three poems that night in a burst of expression and I *absolutely* remember the wild buzzing feeling of having *created something*. Something that felt real and slightly secret, something that expressed ideas and held *meaning*—not just to my budding activist self, but to, like, *mankind*.

I penned the poems first in the back pages (which felt secretive, stealth) of my new mature black faux-leather journal (as in: not a chintzy diary covered in tiny hearts or a spiral-bound Lisa Frank unicorn explosion). Handwriting neat, poems perfectly centered on the soft white pages. Then, once I'd composed them and reread them and marveled at myself, Young Bard that I was, I typed up each one on the electric typewriter (no Macintosh II quite yet) that I'd received for my fifteenth birthday (because I wanted to be a writer and having a typewriter was obviously a thing that a writer needed to have).

Three thin clean sheets of typing paper, now emblazoned with My Truths. Some twenty-five-ish years later, I'm looking back with a kind of mocking self-deprecation and low-key embarrassment. But also: I see something in these poems that makes me happy. I cringe when I read them because now I *am* a Grown-Up Writer, and I am not and have never been a poet—always fiction and nonfiction—and as someone who has taught creative writing to hundreds of young people I have seen poetry written by thirteen-year-olds that is ten billion times more eloquent, real, and nuanced than these.

But! In these poems, I see myself working to become the person that I am today. Someone who, though writing, addresses justice and feminism and resilience and resistance. I still use humor and imagery and I still pay careful attention to rhythm and sound and language (rhyming, not so much). And I guess I am, to some degree, still addressing the Cruel World and the complexities of human consciousness, as I did in these teenage gems.

So behold, dear reader, I share these poems with you, straight from my 1994 journal:

(untitled)

burning air,
fiery heart
smear some paint
call it art.
speak what they want,
think what they don't
believe in something because I won't
speak up child—
—but don't offend,
broken hearts eventually mend
bloody streets,
bloody skies
open your heart. . .
silence the cries
stand up tall—be strong + fight
but sit down quick
if you don't think
right

1994
Ah, young activist. So much to say! And also this:

Glasses

. . . is my yellow your blue?
who the hell am I talking to?
when we touch do we feel the same?
do we play the same damn game?
if I draw a circle do you see a square?
do you know that we're breathing the same stale air?
I hear myself—loud and clear
when I feel joy do you feel fear?
love is strong they all said. . .
can I think when I am dead?
the world is grey and so is your face
I'm suffocating in this sh*tty place

OH MY GOD I *LOVED* THAT LAST LINE. My first swear word in a poem! And can you tell I was reading Thoreau and Whitman? I had a tattered copy of *On Civil Disobedience* and a children's edition of "Song of Myself" and I'm pretty sure that those, combined with the Smiths and Tori Amos, were my biggest influences here. (Also maybe Dickinson because look—at my use!—of em-dashes).

And finally, this one:

Canadian Bridge

it makes no sense
I'm totally lost
my mind is frozen—permafrost
please unfreeze it
I need to think
is leather just as bad as mink?
people feel too much guilt
but I'll cross that bridge after it's been built
—that's a lie—
a blatant one
that bridge will never ever be done
keep on building,
it'll only fall down
and when we cross it we will drown

Here's the thing: I was nowhere near as depressed and morose as these poems might lead you to believe. I was pretty fierce, and definitely getting tuned in to big ideas about oppression and capitalism and feminism—but I wasn't as angsty as I seem in these poems. I was exploring an exaggerated Self. I basked in my creative glory. And then my mom knocked on my door.

"What are you up to?" she inquired, in that casual-but-not-casual mom voice that I definitely use now on my own daughter.

"Oh, just writing some poetry."

Beat.

"Poetry?"

"Yeah. On my typewriter." No big deal. Just a teen writin' some poems.

"Well can I. . . read them?"

Beat. Mild panic.

"Sure." Hands Mom pages, sits back down on carpet. Heart races. Palms sweat. Panic brain.

My mom stood there and read each poem, and the worry radiated from her face. She didn't even have to say it—I could tell what she was thinking about her precious happy daughter—but she did.

"Are you. . . *okay*? Is something wrong? Are you depressed? I—these are just—so—I mean—are you *okay*?"

I took a deep breath and steadied myself. Looked up at my mom and said something that I would say many, many more times over the years. "Of course I'm okay, Mom. It's not necessarily real. I'm *a writer*."

She handed me the poems and backed away, not convinced of my mental health, but clear, I think, on the importance of respecting me and my moody self-expression. And for that, I thank her. And I still do.

Kate Schatz is the author of the New York Times *bestsellers* Rad American Women A–Z, *and* Rad Women Worldwide, *as well as* My Rad Life: A Journal *and* Rid of Me: A Story. *She lives and writes in the Bay Area with her two kids, her dude, and her giant cat. Her angsty poems and other teenage works were all penned in San Jose, where she grew up.*

That Moment I Knew I'd Messed Up

AYAA S.

AGE 16 · INDEPENDENCE HIGH SCHOOL

That moment, I knew I'd messed up. I was sitting on the couch. I realized how bad the situation was. I felt like I was a screw-up. My mom was screaming at me while she was holding my transfer paper, acting as if it were a death threat. I had to give myself a reality check. I realized the path I was going down wasn't the right way to go. A few days before school started, I got a call from my new teacher. She was really nice over the phone. I was actually comfortable asking her questions.

Finally, the first day at my new school. I was fifteen minutes early. I was nervous. My heart was racing. I walked in to find no one in the classroom but my teacher. What I saw was a woman with blue curly hair with the nicest voice and a warm smile that gave out the best vibe. This person was my teacher. From the first greeting and smile, I knew she was someone I could get along with. I felt relief and comfort. I finally found a teacher that would try to understand me before she judged me. I found a great environment at my school and a supportive community. We have an all-female administration, and they are very welcoming. That's not something you find everywhere.

Because of this, my grades improved. I feel better and I'm letting go of my troubled past. I never knew a new school, new teacher, and environment could change me as a person. Now I have the best grades of my life and a teacher I love and trust. My mom is the proudest she's ever been of me.

Ayaa wrote this piece during a Podcasting Field Trip at the 826 Valencia Tenderloin Center. In this program, classes come to our center from all over the city during the school day to write, edit, and record professional podcasts, and learn how to craft an engaging personal story and read it with confidence. Check out 826 Valencia's Message In a Bottle on SoundCloud to hear more!

The Place You Left Me

NAOMI S.

AGE 15 · NEWARK MEMORIAL HIGH SCHOOL

I said it, please don't forget it.
I built up enough courage,
so why is it that you think it's something I'll regret?
I identify with the men
who chopped off their sex organs
and taped them on their chest,
because being black and male in this world
was just too difficult.
I identify with the little girl who puts on basketball shorts
instead of a dress for her seventh birthday,
while her mother hibernates in the kitchen,
praying to all the gods that her little girl isn't gay,
that this is just a phase that'll pass like the seasons.
My life provider
thinks he's my decider.
He talks about what society will do to me,
as if I'm a box of recalled produce.
I wish he'd understand my desire in life
isn't to have mass appeal,
but self thrill.
To have an identity and to identify are two different things.
Identity is an opinionated perspective given to you at birth,
by society;
to identify is a self-driven action.

Yes Mom, Pop,
I identify with lesbian.

This does not mean—I'll be a strung out freak
in a Motel 6.
This does not mean I'm not
human.
Please understand—
I've walked in places where trouble was me,
I've roamed in spaces where there was no light.
You can read my future off my palm,
beat me with sticks
till my skin turns purple and blue,
but never will I ever walk backwards into the place
you left me.

Naomi wrote this poem in the 2014 Young Authors' workshop at 826 Valencia, in which students spend two weeks writing in a variety of forms, hearing from guest speakers, workshopping and revising their work. This poem was published in the chapbook Reaching For This Name *and in* the 826 Quarterly, *vol. 21.*

Inside the Head of a Lonely Fifteen-Year-Old

MEGHAN EPLETT

When I was fifteen my family moved from upstate New York to Wisconsin and my only brother went to college. I was extremely lonely and my room became my refuge. I found comfort in movies, books, and TV shows—imagining ridiculous scenarios for myself that were far more exciting than being a sad teenager with no friends. Also, my self-loathing was peaking—I was insanely worried about my appearance, future, boys, being cool. . . the list goes on. I think in some ways this time in my life fueled my creativity and made me the person I am today—my fifteen-year-old self would be pleasantly surprised.

Meghan Eplett is an art director and illustrator living in Brooklyn.

INSIDE THE HEAD OF A LONELY 15 YEAR OLD

WHO HATES LEAVING HER ROOM.

Scary Home

SARAI H.

AGE 10 · CÉSAR CHÁVEZ ELEMENTARY SCHOOL

Hi, I am a fifteen-year-old girl known as Sarai. Life is not so great in this creepy world. Beverly Hills High School is very exotic.

I am in Ms. Langley's class, and she has always seemed a little off. She seems like she keeps staring at me, like something is wrong. Not that many people know her because there are only six students in the class. Something cold keeps touching me on my shoulder. Every time I enter the room I feel like something bizarre has entered it. It gives me the shivers and I feel really creeped out.

After dismissal, I get my phone and text my friend: "Is your dad going to pick me up from school?" I forgot to mention to you that it is dark in the hall where I am and there are some lights flickering.

My friend writes back, "No," and I say, "Okay." I decide to walk home.

I start getting this feeling, like someone is watching me. I look back and there is an old lady asking for money. I say, "No, sorry," and she gives me this creepy smirk. I'm now on Acorn Street and I have arrived home. I sit on the creaky, old chair.

My mom asks, "How was school?"

"It was good, as always."

My mom cooks my favorite meal, salmon and mashed potatoes. The salmon looks soggy. I tell my mom that I'm not hungry and go to my room. Then I get a message from an unknown number that has my area code. I text back, "Who is this?"

They answer back, "Guess."

I answer, "Give me a hint."

They say, "Look out your window."

"No."

"I can see you," they type.

I say, "I'm not dealing with this craziness. Whoever this is I'm blocking you."

"I warned you," they say.

"Whatever that means," I answer.

I'm scared, and what makes it creepier is that now it's nighttime. Then I hear this eerie noise, and water starts to come out of the walls. I run downstairs and I say, "It's the pipes, the pipes exploded!"

"I'll call the repair store," my mom says.

When the repair people arrive, they go to my room to fix it, which means I need to sleep on the couch alone in the night. When it's bedtime, I say to myself, *Now, how bad could it be?* I forgot to mention that we have windows that are semicircles, so it's creepy because it looks like two eyes looking at you.

I turn over to the other side, but I get the same feeling, like someone is watching me. I look toward the window and the old lady was resting her chin on her arms and looking at me with this distinctive look. I scream and blink a lot and then she disappears.

Then I hear a sound like someone is dragging something big. I open the door and see nothing.

Well, as you can see, my life is horrifying.

Sarai has come to 826 Valencia on a field trip with her class and participated in Exploring Words Summer Camp. She likes to illustrate and wants to be an author when she grows up (and she already is!).

Future Self

SOPHIA M.

AGE 9 · CÉSAR CHÁVEZ ELEMENTARY SCHOOL

Dear Sophia,

Since you're fifteen, what is it like? You're probably bigger than your nine-year-old self. Do you think you can go to Hawaii or Peru during the summer? And did you change your future job, veterinarian? Did you figure out if your mom was lying about being allergic to all animals? I hope you're not getting in trouble. I hope you're doing good in school. I hope you still know how to do gymnastics. Do you know how to speak in Chinese and Japanese?

P.S. Don't think that just because I'm nine, I didn't know what to write.

Sophia wants to be a veterinarian when she grows up (at least for now). She has worked with 826 Valencia at Exploring Words Summer Camp.

Metamorphosis

JOEL H.

AGE 15 · JOHN O'CONNELL HIGH SCHOOL

My name—my name was the first to go. I was staring wistfully out the window, driving to school. As I watched the trees cruise by, unchanging in their roots, I wondered about myself and my life up until then. I was discovering that I didn't feel content with myself, especially my name. My name: the name that was always too long and culturally complex for most everyone to understand, the name that made me the butt of all the jeers and mockeries I'd experience for the rest of my life. I wanted a new name, one that was normal, one that blended in with the rest of society. A name that didn't feel like trying to swallow a bag of dice, that clinked and crumbled down your throat and choked you into a forced moniker, a deadly gamble. I realized I wasn't like the other girls; I didn't like dresses, I hated the onslaught of pink and glitter. I'd rather play with the boys, but they didn't want to play with me. I felt left out, that no one wanted me around. I was in kindergarten, and I was already wishing that I wasn't me.

Fast-forward to second or third grade. That same name was being called, over and over, when my teachers took roll. And over and over, louder and louder, my name was being mocked and parroted maliciously back into my head by my peers. They cut and pasted what should have been an honorable bookmark of heritage and culture into an abomination of a pun. I begged them through tears to stop defacing my identity, to just leave me alone with what dignity I had left. They didn't listen, and the bullying just got worse. It didn't help that I was overweight, which augmented my hell of an academic life.

The bullying wasn't just restricted to the school halls. No matter what I tried to do to make me feel better about myself, I could never escape the pain and torment my family put me through. My behavior was unacceptable for a "young lady" like me. I had to be dainty, yet dignified. I was looked down upon when I wore pants instead of skirts; anything that wasn't bought in the girl's aisle in stores was bought with hesitant hands, as if my family were holding a ticking time bomb in the shape of a dinosaur toy. I was swept under with wave upon wave of jewelry and cosmetics; Mother didn't expect a daughter and saw me as a blessing, perhaps as a way for her to live her dreams through me. She nagged about, as mothers do, but this time her crowing became louder and louder, circling me like a misandrist buzzard. She kept complaining to me about the men in her life, and men in general. Once again, I felt pressured into my prison of femininity.

Several years later, I sought out a social renaissance. Middle school was my transition period. I was free to dress how I liked, to say what I wanted to, and to even have a few male comrades on my side. The bullying stopped, although I was buffeted with its aftermath: depression and anxiety. Although I was coming out of my shell of predestined identity, I was digging myself deeper into confusion. Now that I was free from authoritative decisions, I didn't know who—or what—I was. All I knew was that I didn't like the old me, and I wanted to find out what the new me would be called. In my freshman year of high school, I finally found my word: *transgender*.

This term has been the epicenter of confusion and mockery, often forgotten and ignored entirely by supporters of the LGBTQ community. *Transgender* is an umbrella term used for individuals who do not conform to traditional gender roles and will usually make the changes necessary to achieve their ideal identity. Often it is confused with the term *transvestite*, or the more derogatory term, *tranny*. Contrary to popular belief, these words are not synonymous. Transvestites are simply more on the side of cross-dressers and drag queens. This is something more recreational compared to something life-changing, something that can literally change your physique.

A blog thread discussing the LGBTQ community explains that one of the reasons behind an individual being transgender is their brain chemistry and early brain development. Studies have shown unusual hormone "imbalances," where the most ubiquitous hormone does not correspond to the individual's sex. It is also shown that the brains of transgender individuals do not share characteristics with brains of cisgender individuals, or people who identify with the sex they were given at birth. Many other factors come into play, including influence from the environment and society, but the basis behind the concept is that the chemical makeup of the brain and its development are the driving force of these changes.

Upon registering this newfound data, I began to piece myself together, having more clarity in my life. It certainly explained why I acted differently around my peers, how my thoughts and interests conflicted with those of everyone else. I had always acted masculine for my sex and age, which I thought was normal; therefore, I did things I thought boys liked to do. However, I soon learned that society didn't like masculine figures that spoke in high-pitched voices and wore glitter-spackled shirts with pink kittens on them. They had to be *tougher* and *manlier* than that. Society also didn't like feminine figures who wore shorts and dug around for bugs. Women are too *dainty* and couldn't *possibly* want to get dirty. And when society saw something it didn't like, it lashed out, and it was relentless.

Despite the rough path of discovering who I was going to be, I pushed on. I disregarded the negativity and replaced it with opportunity, finding new doors to open and adding attributes to become who I am today. I sought out advice from other transgender friends on how to be safe while transitioning, and how to break the news to friends and family. With this new radiance and confidence, I feel connected to the world again. I feel less alone with the friends who have stuck with me despite my changes. Which brings about the question: If my friends can accept the way I present myself, why not everyone else? Our world is constantly changing, and to keep up with it, we are also changing. Even if my struggles are unorthodox to others, it is still a journey of finding myself, something just about everyone goes through.

Joel wrote this essay as part of the 2013 Me to We project at John O'Connell High School. In this project, students worked with 826 Valencia tutors to write autobiographical narratives about a group they belong to, with the goal of increasing understanding between writers and readers of different backgrounds. This piece was first published in the chapbook Creatures in the Fog *and in* the 826 Quarterly, *vol. 19.*

Art Kid

LISA BROWN

I was an odd, day-dreamy, bookish kid who loved to draw, stuck in a suburban high school lousy with with hearty, happy preppies. I felt lonely and lost.

When I was fifteen years old, I went to a summer arts program. I found dormfuls of day-dreamy, bookish, and odd art kids. They wore black eyeliner and wrote morose and macabre poetry and listened to punk bands and were happy (though they would *never* admit it). And I was happy because I had found art—painting and drawing and dancing and theater and photography and writing writing writing—and a tribe of art kids. My tribe.

I am still odd, day-dreamy, and bookish. But not lonely and lost: I still have my tribe of art kids. But I don't wear black eyeliner. Well, not every day.

Lisa Brown is an illustrator, writer, and cartoonist. Her most recent books include The Airport Book, Mummy Cat *by Marcus Ewert, and* Goldfish Ghost *by Lemony Snicket. She has been involved with 826 for fifteen years as a supporter, workshop instructor, field trip volunteer, publications contributor, and now board member. Lisa lives in San Francisco.*

DYED
HAIR

SAFETY
PINS

DOC
MARTENS

TIGHTS and SHORTS

THE
SMITHS

SEX PISTOLS

DAVID
BOWIE

ARMY
SURPLUS
BAG

DALI

GOREY

Edward
Gorey

SALINGER

ART KID

Boredom Will Be Teaching Boredom

ANTHONY R.

AGE 12 · DE MARILLAC ACADEMY

Ingredients

3 cups of homework

2 tablespoons of waiting

50 million gallons of lectures about behavior

2½ cups of sleepiness

½ tablespoon of yawning

2 gallons of repeatedly looking at the clock for school to be over

1½ cups of doodling

Directions

In order to be the most bored person ever, start by pouring out fifty million gallons of lectures about behavior. This will help you stop paying attention, like your brain is replaced with a walnut. Now, add in the two tablespoons of waiting, along with the three cups of homework. This will make you whine and groan, like a child wanting a toy. At the same time, level out the two-and-one-half cups of sleepiness and one-half tablespoon of yawning. Adding those ingredients will make sure that you're going to be sleeping like a hibernating bear. Who knows? You'll probably wake up at the same time! Now, in another bowl, add the two gallons of repeatedly looking at the clock. Adding this will be important because you have to make sure that you're going to be driven insane due to a lack of patience, making your head explode like putting Mentos in Coca-Cola. In the same cup, pinch in the one-and-a-half cups of doodling because you have nothing better to do. Then pour the contents of the second bowl into the main bowl and mix it all together. Most importantly, bake it to 99,999,999 degrees, because in that heat you'll be sweating like Niagara Falls in heavy rainfall in April due to impatience. It might be even worse if it is a hot day. Now you're finally finished having the most boring time, and you're even more bored than waiting for a bus that arrives in the year 5047! It will be so boring that boredom will be teaching boredom how to be bored while being bored.

Anthony wrote this recipe for boredom in an After-School Writing Workshop at the 826 Valencia Tenderloin Center. Once a week, students from De Marillac Academy visit the center during their after-school enrichment hour to build their writing skills through creative writing and one-on-one tutoring, polishing everything from to poems to recipes like this one.

The Potato Room

BRIGID M. HUGHES

I spent the summer I was fifteen as a nanny. I had done a lot of babysitting, and at fifteen I considered myself very grown-up in general. So when a family friend and his wife got jobs at a summer camp and asked me to go with them to watch their little girl, I said yes. My parents had taken us on our yearly family vacation to this camp, so we knew it well and they were on board with the plan. Plus I had three other siblings and they really didn't mind having one less around for a few weeks. So this is how, before I had a driver's license or a first kiss, I found myself living on my own in the middle of Yosemite National Park.

The camp itself had been built in the 1920s, a home for loggers and workers constructing the nearby O'Shaughnessy Dam. But it was still about the same as it had been since a bajillion years ago, except for the electricity and the pool. It was one square mile, located four hours away from my home in San Francisco, and it hosted about five hundred people each week, families housed in old wooden cabins with little decks to sit on or to drape your swimsuit out to dry at the end of the day.

The camp had two sides. One had a big lake and a pool, and a huge lawn full of birch trees where people sprawled out on blankets all day. The other side had horse stables and a campfire pit, an office, and a general store with an ice cream parlor. It also had the biggest building, which was a massive dining hall, a cafeteria-style building where folks ate three squares a day and played bingo on Wednesday nights. Each day there was a list of activities for kids, and just after dinner, there were marshmallows or a talent show or a movie night.

I lived in the bunkhouse, an L-shaped wooden building in the middle of camp. The bunkhouse had several rooms along a long hallway, and I shared it with other people working for the camp, some staff cooks and lifeguards and cafeteria dishwashers. Everyone wore shorts and T-shirts and sandals. There was a group bathroom and a few tiny showers with concrete floors. After a few days, no matter how hard you scrubbed, your feet were still dirty.

I lived in the Potato Room. No one was meant to live in the Potato Room. It was small and very hot and it smelled funny, but there was nowhere else to put a fifteen-year-old camp babysitter. I couldn't live with the college kids in the dorms near the baseball field who were lifeguards and servers in the cafeteria, and I couldn't have my own cabin. So someone had squeezed a tiny bed and a dresser in there and gave me my first key to my own place.

I soon found out it was called the Potato Room because for decades it had been used to store the camp's potatoes. From the 1920s until just before I got there, a truck would dump hundreds of potatoes in this room. Then a cook from the kitchen would draw the losing straw and be tasked with peeling them for the day. I could tell from dark stains on the floor where the dry ones had been stacked, and where the wet ones landed. The room still smelled like potatoes, of earth and dirt and roots, of things that still grew and sprouted even after they've been pulled from the ground.

The room had one square window, a little curtain, and one overhead bulb. Every night, a constant firework of moths and wings and antennae bounced against the bare, yellow-tinted bulb. During the day, the room got direct sunlight. Just walking in there made the middle of my back sweat. On those first nights I rolled a big bulky sleeping bag onto the cot and in the morning I rolled it back up and fluffed up my pillow and felt like the luckiest girl ever.

But after the first few days, I became weary of this whole living-by-myself thing. I struggled with being alone. The camp had no TV or Internet. There were a few public phones a short bike ride away. Homesickness sprang on me at random times during the day and I cried and cried as quietly as I could in the group bathrooms or into my pillow until I was out of tears. Sometimes after that, I had to go for walks. I took my flashlight and went down to the lake and listened to the bullfrogs burping along the edges of the water.

Babysitting the little girl was the easy part. After breakfast, I took her to make lanyards, or to build sandcastles in the sandbox, or to go to the tiny camp playground and use the swings. Being in charge of her allowed me to do the things a child would want to do, things I still wanted to do but felt like I shouldn't.

I liked eating dinner with the little girl and her parents. They were lovely. He ran the recreation program and she ran the office. They wanted to know my opinion on things, and what movies I liked, and if I had thought about what to major in at college. Adults had not asked me very specific questions before, and I enjoyed thinking about our talks and good answers for next time.

Each week, I made friends with other fifteen- and sixteen-year-olds visiting camp with their families. Most of them complained about it, being stuck there with their parents, how bored they were. I wasn't bored at all, just lonely sometimes, and confused about my place there, but I nodded and agreed that it could be so lame. But they all thought it was cool I was living there alone, and wanted to know what it was like. I told them it was cool. I told them about my room, and about how they put Whirl butter substitute in all the food so you felt full faster and didn't go back for seconds. The girls talked about boyfriends and lip gloss, and the boys dared each other to drag everyone's floating toys and lounge rafts into the lake in the middle of the night.

I played spin the bottle for the first time on the deck of the general store, and the bottle landed on a boy I had a huge crush on. He was blond and tan and athletic and mean to everyone. I was so nervous I kept my eyes closed and ended up kissing his chin. He made fun of me in front of everyone, and I felt an embarrassment I had never really felt before, like a rock in the gut. I hid from that friend group for the last two days, until they all had packed up and left.

Still, aside from a few snafus, I was picking up some good info. I had a crush on one of the staffers who washed dishes and kept his T-shirt sleeves rolled up all the time. This first crush took up a huge amount of time and energy, a new space involving imagining a thousand interactions and flirtations that would never take place but was nevertheless both draining and exhilarating. At dinner, I didn't have to be pulled into conversation. I was actually good at making new friends. After a few weeks I was having a great time. I wasn't afraid anymore. I listened to my music on repeat, and I played it loud from the Potato Room, just like the college kids from the dorms. I read a lot. I went down to the lake by myself every afternoon for a swim to the other side of the blue-green shore. I started telling campers about things going on and what they should do, since I was pretty much an expert now.

By the end of my time, I was bounding up and down the wooden steps of the bunkhouse like anyone else who lived there, and shouting hello to the other workers in camp. One of the staffers showed me how to take some snacks from the dining hall in case I got hungry in my room, and I took lots of short naps, and I figured out when I needed to put some extra sunscreen on my shoulders, and I stayed away from boys who I knew wanted to kiss me but would make fun of me for kissing them. These were important lessons.

Still, at night, when I was lying there alone in the Potato Room, I imagined what it'd be like to have to peel those potatoes all day for everyone, knowing that you couldn't leave until the task was done. I imagined this person sitting just to the left of me in the small space next to the bed, with a potato and a small knife and a stool. This person undertaking this peculiar task alone, with all their thoughts, and the heat, and the funny smell. I felt sorry for this person. Or more specifically, I felt kindred to them. It was no mistake we had both ended up here. All in all, I figured it was probably a lot like being fifteen.

Brigid M. Hughes is a writer and editor. She received her MFA in short fiction and personal essay from the University of San Francisco. Her work has appeared in the Rumpus, Sparkle + Blink, *and* Haighteration. *She has read for 826 Valencia, Quiet Lightning, and Under the Influence.*

To an Expired Dream

LUMING Y.

AGE 17 · LOWELL HIGH SCHOOL

Three years ago, I saw you in the honeyed glaze
of adolescence, and you were my whirlpool,
my optional bullet to the heart.
I knew I could be smothered by the force of your waves,
knew the obstacles no one could face,
but I jumped anyway,
silently, headfirst.
Then I was submerged,
but like the trembling smoothness of rain, it felt right.

Two years ago, you were but a gentle dream,
a cool sprinkling of water droplets
that laid themselves upon my cheek.
I treaded along your castle walls,
but knew you dined with queens, so
I dared not speak.

One year ago, sixteen was sweet like ripe nectar
as I blossomed a sturdy backbone,
as you sprouted relentless wings
and saved lovesick damsels.
But you were still the brightest fantasy,
the sour stream of expired dreams.
If I were bigger, I would have reached you.
If I were better, you would have invited me in,
past your vortex
—but I am not, and our time is spent.

Years have flown by with the current,
water slows and chugs along, repetitively,
prepared to stop.

But before the waters calm, before the world moves on,
be quiet.
Be with me.
Let me feel the waves pound at the edges of our whirlpool,
throwing rivers in the heavy air
as it crumbles, melts, into soft ocean
and our boundaries disappear.
Make me infinite,
as if the world is just two mismatched orphans,
as if we had a chance to say hello
before nature forced a goodbye.

Luming wrote this poem in the 2015 Young Authors' Workshop at 826 Valencia, in which students spend two weeks writing in a variety of forms, hearing from guest speakers, workshopping and revising their work. This poem was published in the chapbook Each Blaring Hue *and in* the 826 Quarterly, *vol. 23.*

Diverse Voices of a Onetime Shameful Girl

TIFFANI W.

AGE 15 · JOHN O'CONNELL HIGH SCHOOL

My elementary school was predominantly white and I was one of the outsiders. I was the only "Lasian" (Latina and Asian) girl there and I felt so ashamed of my language and wondered why I couldn't blend in like the other kids. They would have the same generic lunch, culture, and vacations, and I was different.

My family would come pick me up from school and speak to me in Spanish, which caused stares and made me feel embarrassed every single time it would happen. My face would turn tomato red and I wouldn't want anyone to look at me.

Why would I get like this, you ask? I don't distinctly remember why, but I felt the pressure to be "normal" and the same. At lunch I would have homemade food, such as traditional dishes like *arroz con pollo*, and everybody else would have the same old peanut butter and jelly sandwich and juice box. I always felt like the big elephant in the room that nobody wanted to talk about.

At the time I didn't realize I had true wealth in the form of family support, culture, and my bilingual ability, but it is something I have grown up to realize and take pride in.

My family is from Nicaragua and they're naturally very loud and very proud in their culture. "*Siempre tengas orgullo en ser latina!*" my uncle would say.

He always reminds me how important it is to not be ashamed of who we are. He would say there is dignity in being part of a loving culture and community. I have to say, Nicaraguans are some of the most proud people I've been around. They always love to talk about their country and different traditions. Once they start, they don't stop—trust me. I didn't really realize that until I was older, but when I was younger I thought they were obnoxious and annoying.

I don't mind it as much now, and genuinely enjoy being with them. I didn't really appreciate my family, even though when we all were together we'd have such a great time.

My family is quite big, which is something I wasn't very fond of. I would constantly get annoyed with them and just remember their loud voices talking about who married and who did what. I thought a big family was a hassle, but I learned to embrace it, and found it entertaining to meet various uncles and aunts that I can get to know and build relationships with.

Something my mom would always say in Spanish is, "Family is forever." I would respond with, "Why?" and she would say, "Family will always be there for you in times of need and will always be by your side when life isn't going your way."

When I was small I didn't really take that to heart, but now it's something that has stuck with me. I've been through thick and thin with my family, but throughout all my struggles, they've always been there for me to support me, and once I took note of that, it has never left me.

Spanish has always been prominent in my life. "You can't roll your *R*s?" my mom would say with a look of embarrassment on her face. "I'm trying!" I'd reply.

Spanish was my first language and I turned out to be one of the kids that understood it well, but when I spoke I couldn't pronounce things that well. My family would make fun of me and it would contribute to the sense of humiliation I felt toward my language. I enjoyed speaking it and still do to this day, but when I was younger I felt like it was a hurdle that I struggled to jump over.

I still struggle with pronouncing things, but I don't care anymore and enjoy learning new things, instead of getting annoyed when I would have to practice my Spanish rather than English. Without being able to speak Spanish, I wouldn't be able to communicate with my family, who are very important people in my life (even though they made fun of me occasionally). They have consistently encouraged me to practice Spanish and take pride in and acknowledge my bilingualism, which has allowed me to communicate with various people. That is something I didn't acknowledge when I was younger.

I was about nine years old when I was at the peak of my embarrassment. When I got home, I only wanted to be called white and American. I just wanted to fit in and not be looked at weirdly all the time. Once I was at lunch and my mom came and dropped off my food, which I forgot at home. When I opened my container, which had *carne asada* and *tostones*, the other kids had no idea what it was and just made fun of me for having gross food even if they had never tried it before. Ever since that day, I was so self-conscious of my lunch and what people thought of what I brought.

At the time I would constantly get in arguments with my parents about wanting to be called an American. I didn't realize that if you lived in America, you were American.

My fourth-grade self was a little ignorant, I'd have to say. I didn't really like it when people called me Nicaraguan. I felt so different and excluded. I would get in these arguments almost every week and just feel so ashamed about who I was. I just wanted to be like everyone else and not be the extraterrestrial that I appeared to be. At the time I didn't realize that the wealth I possessed from growing up in a bilingual and culturally rich household would benefit me so much in the future.

As I got older I learned to appreciate these wonderful things and take pride in who I was. I'm still going through my burst of embracing, which is something I'm enjoying in my life right now.

Last year, when I started to go to a school mostly populated by Latinos, I began to appreciate my secondary language a lot more. Especially when I took an ethnic studies class last year, which allowed me to open my mind further and become more knowledgeable in different cultures and accepting of my bilingualism. The class talked about various topics. One of the topics was identity, and as the whole class discussed it, I slowly began to admire myself more and became proud to be a person of color.

I really had no pride or appreciation for my culture at all. I was ashamed and very embarrassed of who I was and wanted to fit in so badly. I argued all the time about my identity, but never stopped to realize my identity was something that made me unique and culturally rich.

My language and family have played big roles in my life and have shaped me in various ways, and quite frankly it was something I did not acknowledge earlier. I've been learning to embrace myself for a while and it's really great. I've been practicing my Spanish more and asking more about my family roots, which is great. Also, my ability to speak two languages is something very beneficial for me. I have better job opportunities, can communicate with a large variety of people, and overall have an advantage academically.

I have become very appreciative of my ability and always take on opportunities that will further help me speak Spanish. I have come to know many people who have encountered the same situation as me and agree that throughout all the embarrassment you face and bumps along the way, it feels way better to learn to love yourself.

Even if you haven't fully learned or learned just a little, it's something. As we all know, everybody is different, and the journey toward self-acceptance may vary.

Once I came to find people who shared a similar experience with me, it felt enjoyable and reassuring to have people who understood what I was saying and what I went through. We all learn from our mistakes and struggles, but it's never too late to identify them and become more educated and treasure what we have in our lives.

Tiffani wrote this essay as part of the 2015 Cultural Wealth project at John O'Connell High School. In this project, students worked with 826 Valencia tutors to write autobiographical narratives about what makes them "culturally wealthy"—what aspects of their identities hold value that might sometimes be overlooked. This poem was published in the chapbook Let It Out, Speak Freely, and Don't Be Afraid *and in the 826 Quarterly, vol. 23.*

MORE IN COMMON THAN WE MIGHT LIKE TO THINK

ADVICE FOR BEING FIFTEEN AND BEYOND

The Puzzle

JESSE G.

AGE 15 · THURGOOD MARSHALL HIGH SCHOOL

A'ight, listen.

Let's unfold the truth like a picture made of puzzle pieces.
This world's purpose is to work,
keep pockets filled with riches.
Everyone has their story,
leaving them with battle stitches.
A soldier coming back home from war,
mind broken, stolen, killed for a country,
and a boy taking care of his mother,
sick and ill due to a car crash
that left her silent forever
Yeah, where's the wishes?
Wishes of doing the right thing and making all the bad go away.
I'm flinching.
Life has many choices, but it keeps on switching.
Think before you make decisions.
I learned that the hard way.
You're not aiming for no collision.
That's your mission.
Envision yourself being great.
"If someone else, why can't you?"
It's not destiny nor fate.
You choose what road to go.
Time to set your mind straight.
Activate the lion inside us all, meditate.
Roar and say, "This is my life!"
It's not impossible doing what's right.

Darkness can't harm us anymore.
The light—it's just too bright.
With all your might,
stand, you can fight
The puzzle is completed.

Jesse wrote this poem in a Podcasting Field trip at the 826 Valencia Tenderloin Center. In this program, classes come to our center from all over the city during the school day to write, edit, and record professional podcasts, and learn how to craft an engaging personal story and read it with confidence. Check out 826 Valencia's Message in a Bottle *on SoundCloud to hear more!*

Fifteen Things I Learned When I Was Fifteen That Turned Out to Be True

DANIEL HANDLER

1. If you're someplace where you have to give your name to pick something up, give a goofy name, so when your hamburger is ready they'll say "Lampshade! Medium-rare hamburger for Lampshade!"

2. Coats should have a lot of pockets.

3. If someone says something insulting to you, pause for a moment and blink at them before replying quietly, in order to drive them nuts. You can say, "Thank you for your interest." I took that from an old movie and it really works. "Your shirt looks stupid." Blink, blink. "Thank you for your interest."

4. Dancing is ridiculous. There's no such thing as being a "good dancer" unless you're talking about ballet or something. If you like a song, turn up the volume and just move your body however you want to. The other dancers aren't thinking about you really. Everybody is paying attention to themselves 95 percent of the time.

5. Everybody is paying attention to themselves 95 percent of the time. My mom told me this and she was totally thinking of herself when she said it.

6. When someone is offended, apologize as promptly and sincerely as you can muster, even when you think it's not entirely your fault or perhaps not your fault at all. If it is really the fault of the person who is offended, apologize even more. Don't do it sarcastically. Just apologize.

7. If you're a picky eater, for whatever reason, don't talk about it all the time.

8. Your friends are important. Keep them. Keep in touch. Forgive them because they don't know what they're doing and they're confused, just like you. Tell them you miss them and you're thinking of them. Wish them luck when they need luck. Walk around with them listening to their problems. When other people are mean to them, side with your friends. Say things like "I can't believe she said that to you! She's a monster! I'm going to kick her and steal her bicycle and light all her shirts on fire for you!" Don't do it, of course, but keep talking like that. "I'm going to get a bunch of really old apple juice and spill it on her. She's awful! How can we give her pimples?"

9. Bathe. Take a shower. People smell more often than they think they do. If you're not sure if you need to shower, just take a shower and scrub your armpits.

10. Send people funny things in the mail. Rip an ugly picture out of a catalog and write "This is the most beautiful sweater I've ever seen in my life" on it and put it in an envelope and mail it to a friend. Don't just do it with your phone because everything is funnier in an envelope.

11. Take a lot of notes.

12. Be super nice to waiters and baristas and the secretary at the office and anybody with a hard job.

13. You're never sorry you brought a book.

14. When someone mentions someone who upsets you, pretend for a second that you don't know who they're talking about. "Lorraine? Oh, *Lorraine*. Right. Gosh, I haven't thought of Lorraine in a long time—so what's up with Lorraine?"

15. Don't tell people your dreams. They're super boring. Instead, tell people what's on your mind. Tell people what has happened to you and what you've seen and heard. Listen to what they say back. Your voice, your story; my voice, my story. This is all there is. There is nothing else.

Daniel Handler is the author of six novels, most recently All the Dirty Parts, *and, as Lemony Snicket, far too many books for children. He lives in San Francisco and fell in love with 826 Valencia before it was born.*

Making Yourself Small: A Beginner's Guide

BLAISE K.

AGE 15 · GATEWAY HIGH SCHOOL

One: Be flexible. Flexibility is important for folding yourself up to stay hidden, keeping it fun for them, and making sure you are never commanding.

Two: Never be commanding. Commanding is demanding, is for controlling girls, strong girls, and independent women. The girls with greedy lungs, the unwanted ones.

Three: Practice saying no. As in: When you need something that would inconvenience them, say no to it. When something could make things easier for you but would take away from their good time, say no to it too, because God forbid you just want to go slow. When you find something that makes you smile but, you know, it's just, like, maybe too much of a hassle? Say no. But still, sometimes don't. When no, you don't want that, no you don't like that—

Four: Practice saying yes. Because yes, they want that, yes, they like that, and yes, they've convinced themselves they need that. Give them that. As in, forget that you exist too, as more than just the moon to their sun, as more than just a ghost that shines only when graced by their godly light. They might have a mean streak but that doesn't give you permission to bite. Accept them as a beautiful mess, as dominance in excess, don't try to change them. Just say yes.

Five: Smile. Smile even though your heart is aching, even though it's breaking with every sour word they speak at you, every wrongly placed punch they throw at you. Smile even though your feet are blistered and your shins are bruised, your knees are bleeding and you're beginning to feel used. Smile because it makes them happy and you pretty, and maybe if you're pretty and you get a little ditzy you won't have to try so hard to be witty.

Six: Resent the world for making you like this. Resent yourself for going along with it. Resent because you don't have anything else to spend but you are not short of reasons to repent, to beg. Maybe you were simply born for this torment.

Seven: Explode. Because in this existence you can only get so small. Explode loudly and proudly so that no one can ignore you. Put no one else before you in your own mind, your own life. To hell with it all. Act as the big bang and expand into the universe of you. Let the dust settle into mountains and let hills roll from your fingertips. Water the seeds that have been waiting, covered in dirt, rinse away all the hurt, and let them grow. It's the only way you'll let some life in.

Blaise wrote this piece in the Writing and Publishing Apprentices Workshop at 826 Valencia, which she has participated in for two years. Blaise's work has been published in several 826 Valencia chapbooks and in the 826 Quarterly, *vol. 24.*

Fifteen Things I Would Like to Tell My Fifteen-Year-Old Self

THAO NGUYEN

1. Don't worry, soon you will discover that you can layer your hair.

2. Your mom had to start a new life, in a new country, in a new language. Try to understand how hard that would be and be so proud of her.

3. Spend time with your grandmother. Really talk to her and ask her questions.

4. Your nose is not too flat, and do not pay any attention to all the talk about getting the double eyelid surgery.

5. There is nothing wrong with not being white.

6. There is nothing wrong with being Vietnamese.

7. There is nothing weak about being a girl.

8. It's totally fine that you don't want to hang out in your friend's basement and watch boys play video games. Do not go. Stay home and keep playing guitar. You are not missing out on anything. Anything.

9. The reason you love *Party of Five* so much is you have a crush on Charlie's on-again/off-again girlfriend, Kirsten, played by Paula Devicq.

10. Do not hang out with people who make you feel bored or bad.

11.   If it feels unsafe, get out of there.

12.   Go outside more.

13.   Have more confidence in your physical strength.

14.   Your instincts are to be kind, do not go against them.

15.   You have good ideas.

Thao Nguyen is a songwriter, musician, and the frontwoman of Thao & the Get Down Stay Down. She lives in San Francisco and has been a volunteer at 826 Valencia since 2010.

Four Steps to Being Me

SOFIYA W.

AGE 15 · RAOUL WALLENBERG TRADITIONAL HIGH SCHOOL

First, question everything. Make up stories on how the world works, why leaves are green or maybe why your brothers are so irritating. Keep a journal (very important) and write things like your day, your month, or your year. How's school? How's life? How's Earth? Et cetera, et cetera. Make sure you write down anything that's stuck in your head, like the lyrics of that Nirvana song you forgot the name of, or five reasons why Thor will always be your favorite Avenger.

Second, attempt to change the way you think from time to time, but always revert back to your old self by the end of the day. Be modest at certain times and arrogant at others. Always respect your teachers, especially the ones who give out mini donuts for every question you get right. Constantly think about what others think of you, then immediately scold yourself for caring so much. Make a fuss about doing the dishes, then remind yourself that your mom works hard enough without you throwing a fit, and feel guilty. Create a video dedicated to annoying your older brother and have your best friend cohost it with you; make sure you wake up extra early just so you can scare him out of his sleep.

Third, be extremely competitive. Have an arm-wrestling match in the middle of science class when the teacher isn't looking. Wonder how you are compared to others and feel sad when someone is better than you.

Finally, feel proud when someone compliments your writing. Be delighted when your favorite Muse song pops up on Pandora. Feel excited when you think of your future as a fashion designer, CEO, toxicologist, or whatever you feel like being at the moment. Dream about what it would be like to be a child genius, a music prodigy, or an Oscar-winning actor; be glad that you're not.

Sofiya wrote and revised this piece in the 2013 Young Authors' Workshop at 826 Valencia, in response to the prompt, "write a series of instructions for how to be you." The piece was published first in the chapbook How To Be Us *and again in* the 826 Quarterly, *vol. 19.*

You Were There for Me from the Get

SAMANTHA P.

AGE 17 · DOWNTOWN HIGH SCHOOL

You were there for me from the get. . . You understand me in such a mysterious way since we're complete opposites. You go to church, family functions, you wake up extra early for seminary before school. I cringe at the idea of waking up early, I barely go to church now, and I barely go see my family because I am trying to graduate on time.

You attend Burton, I go to Downtown High. You are going to a four-year, and I'm headed to City. You live in Bernal, I live in the Rich. You, more than anyone, know my struggle, but you appreciate the beauty of it. When I am down and out, you tell me, "Girl, do you know who you are? Put on some hoops, throw on some lashes, and DO YOU!"

See, that is typical Asia language. When you say that, I know that means, "You are blessed. Get it together, or I am going to smack you across the face to make you remember."

I've had a lot of friends throughout the years, but they've all disappeared as fast as they came. But you are not just a friend. When I hear "blood makes you related but loyalty makes you family," I think of you. Through the ups and downs, you've been there, picking up the pieces.

We fell out for a couple months but fell right back in like we never left. My *rida*. You make me process real-life situations and humble me quick! We are not perfect, but we don't try to be. I don't mind you coming to my house 'cause you know wassup. I got hella people living there, and you don't mind because it's the same thing on your side. You don't judge, and I don't either, 'cause God don't like ugly.

You were there for me from the get.

Samantha wrote and performed this monologue in 2015 as part of the Acting for Critical Thought project at Downtown High School. Students wrote monologues and plays about resistance and resilience, worked with 826 Valencia tutors, and took acting classes each week with the American Conservatory Theater. This monologue was published in the chapbook Judged at First Sight *and in* the 826 Quarterly, *vol. 23.*

A Letter to My Fifteen-Year-Old Self

SARAH SAX

I grew up in a family of bookworms. While my sister was poring through Russian lit, I devoured my dad's collection of Donald Duck, Asterix, and Lil' Abner anthologies. When translated manga showed up in my local bookstore, I was hooked. I read, analyzed, and redrew every panel of every book in my collection. My love for comics and cartoons shaped my identity as a budding artist. I filled sketchbook after sketchbook with my sketches and stories.

By age fifteen, my peers were shifting away from *Sailor Moon* and Harry Potter. I still loved the things they were rejecting, but I was self-conscious about expressing that love. It felt like I hadn't gotten the memo about how to "grow up." By the time I started college, I was hiding my old sketchbooks and seeking an adulthood I didn't really understand.

Over time, I've grown to embrace fifteen-year-old-me for who I was: someone who was motivated to create, to engage, and to cultivate my interests. I've worked hard to develop a personal practice that fosters that sense of joy in creation without shame. I'm motivated by a broader set of influences than when I was fifteen, but I still make room for a heavy rotation of new comics and cartoons.

Sarah Sax is an Oakland-based illustrator and animator. She has a background in arts education and works in technology illustrating for games and apps. In her spare time, she writes comics about baseball and creates pillows shaped like cats. She's been volunteering with 826 Valencia since 2014 as a Field Trips illustrator. In 2015, Sarah's illustrations were featured in the 826 Valencia coloring book Let's Get Pizza Instead.

A LETTER TO MY 15-YEAR-OLD-SELF
BY SARAH SAX
Hey Sarah!
I know you're in the middle of perfecting your original manga character, but this will only take a minute:
Right now you love the things you love...
SCRITCHA SCRITCH
...without shame.
crumple
crumple
But soon you'll be embarrassed by your loves that feel too "kiddie."
TAP! TAP! TAP!
HARRY POTTER
GOLDEN COMPASS
PETER PAN
So I'm writing to remind you:
HARRY POTTER
GOLDEN COMPASS
PETER PAN
Be kind to yourself.
Embrace your inner nerd and all that she loves.
Don't shy away from new loves. Both the old and new shape you and push you to grow.
But give yourself permission to feel proud of the things you love.
And feel proud of the things your love inspires you to create.
It's a lot more rewarding to follow your interests than to spend your energy worrying about how to be a grown up.
Besides, when you become grown up (and care less about what people think) you'll get a lot of mileage out of your of Sailor Moon knowledge. ♥
SCRIBBLE
SCRIBBLE
SCRIBBLEE
SCRIBBLE
SCRIBBBLE
SCRIBBLE
SCRIBBLE
SCRIBBLLEE
SCRIBBLE
SCRIBBLE
SCRIBBLE
SCRIBBLE
SCRIBBLE
Love Always, Sarah

When I'm Fifteen Years Old...

KIMBERLY A.

AGE 9 · BUENA VISTA HORACE MANN K-8

When I'm fifteen, I want to be a famous YouTuber. I want to make videos of DIY slime, toys, my adventures, and pranks. I want to have one thousand subscribers. Here are some of my DIY slime recipes:

Slime

Ingredients: glue, borax with hot water, food coloring.
You have to wait until the borax dissolves to pour it into the glue. Then mix it all together.

Fuzzy Slime

Ingredients: glue, shaving cream, contact solution, food coloring
You have to pour the contact solution bit by bit until everything sticks together.

Butter Slime

Ingredients: Yoplait yogurt, flour
Pour the flour bit by bit until it gets soft.

Crunchy Slime

Ingredients: glue, borax with hot water, beads

Glitter Slime

Ingredients: glue, borax with hot water, glitter of different colors or one color

Rainbow Slime

Ingredients: glue, borax with hot water, rainbow food coloring

Pearl Slime

Ingredients: glue, borax with hot water, lots of pearls

Transparent Slime

Ingredients: transparent glue, borax with hot water

I also want to make videos of me showing my toys to the camera. I also want to take videos of my adventures. The last thing I want to take videos of is pranks. For example, I could surprise my brother with a puppy, and he will think it's his and that he has to take care of it and keep it, but it belongs to someone else.

Kimberly has visited 826 Valencia on a field trip with her school and participated in Exploring Words Summer Camp. When she grows up she wants to a YouTuber or a police officer.

Words from a Wise Man

ELIA G.

AGE 15 · MISSION HIGH SCHOOL

My uncle Jorge wasn't the type of guy to be nice. He gave you love his way: the gangster way. He grew up being in a gang. With his friends, he was hard. He never showed any feelings around them, and no love. He would say that he didn't care about life, about anybody. But he was a whole different person when he was with me versus when he was with his friends.

With me, he was caring and loving. He used to show me how much he cared for our family by giving us love and being there for us unconditionally. But people would look at him the wrong way. You could see their eyes narrow as they looked at him, sizing him up, but they just didn't know what an amazing man he was. The streets couldn't see him being "soft," but he was the first love of my life. He raised me tough like a boy, but with love so that my heart would be soft. He was smart and wise.

My uncle Jorge has been my father figure my whole life. I am who I am because of him. He was serious most of the time, but when he was funny, he could make you cry with laughter. He taught me all my values: how to be nice, how to keep on going, and how to try to understand life even when it seems impossible. Most of all, he taught me how to be kind to people no matter what. He said, "Be kind to people; you never know when you will need them. And you can maybe, just maybe, change the world to a better place. To a better tomorrow." To be honest, when he initially said it, I didn't believe him. It sounded stupid at first.

He tried his best to show me what being kind is and what it looks like. I know it was hard for him. He was raised being a "G," and *kind* wasn't in his vocabulary when he was growing up. But he showed me how being kind can put a smile on people's faces, or make their day. I asked him once, "Is being kind a value?" And he said, "No, mija, being kind comes from your heart. It comes from you."

Before he taught me this, I had never been kind to people. I used to believe that if you had a hard heart, it was better because people wouldn't step on you. So it was hard to be kind to others. I used to be really selfish. I would never think of others; everything had to do with me only. Someone would ask me for help or advice, but I would just turn my back on them. When my friend Madeline would come up to me and ask me what she should do about a problem, I would just say, "I don't know," and change the subject. Why? Because if I helped her I wouldn't get anything in return.

But then, one time, one of my friends was going through some stuff. I could tell because she was depressed, and you could see it written all over her face. At first, I didn't know how to help. It wasn't something I thought I could help with. I didn't want to get into her family problems. But this time, I needed to. She was like a sister to me, and I needed to do something for her. I couldn't give her my back. I thought it was going to be difficult, but I started with something as simple as a smile, and I know she felt supported by me. Later on, I heard she did the same thing with someone else. She was there for her friend, like I had been for her. This taught me that if you're kind to someone, that person will probably be kind to someone else who is struggling with something. I thought back to what my uncle said about how kindness can change the world. I realized I had changed the world that day, even if only in a small way.

One act of kindness that I appreciated was when my uncle gave my sister some advice. My sister is three years older than me. She was sixteen at the time. They weren't close, though, and didn't really talk because he thought she was childish for her age. But I told him she was going through some problems with her boyfriend. My uncle told me he was going to be there for her and talk to her.

He was locked up at the time, which meant we had to go down to the jail to see him. When we got there, a lot of people were waiting to see their loved ones. We went at night, and the place was unwelcoming. The jail was a cinder block, dark and chilly, and all you could hear were people's footsteps and the voices of the police officers saying, "Go left," or "Go up the steps." Even though they hadn't been close, when my sister needed some guidance in her life, my uncle was there. He made sure she could count on someone if she was going through a hard time in her life. Things didn't go the way he wanted because she didn't end up taking his advice, but he tried and my sister knew he loved her. Kindness doesn't always work the way you want or expect, but she could keep that memory of our visit in her mind. And sooner or later she would take his advice into consideration.

I don't believe in many things. I mean, what's the point? Isn't the world messed up anyway? I mean, why believe in something if it's not going to change people? And to change the world, we need to change people first. But I was beginning to see that by being kind, I could make people believe in kindness, and in that way, I could change the world.

I believe in God, but not everyone does. Some people don't want to believe in religion. Why? Because there are so many rules. But why not believe in something without rules? In something you can do at any time and everywhere? Being kind to someone is not hard! You don't need money to be kind. You can give a stranger a smile, and that can make that person's day. The world has enough hate already; a little bit of kindness wouldn't be too much to ask for. You can do someone a big favor by telling them they're beautiful or by giving them a hand when they need it. It will come back to you. Just like they say, "What goes around, comes around."

People are unkind because we live in a society with racism, bullying, crime, and hate. Another reason why people are unkind is because they cannot deal with their own problems, and therefore can't deal with someone else's problems. I know for me, if I'm going through some stuff, I don't want to help others because I want to be helped instead. But people should be kind, and I always try to be kind, because it makes us better people and opens more doors in our lives. I believe that kindness can be the key to a better world.

If everyone believed in this, then the world would be a better place. It would be calmer. People would be nicer to each other. There wouldn't be wars, teenagers killing each other, or families destroyed. With more kindness, there wouldn't be so much hate around the world. Can kindness change the world? I don't know for sure, but I think so, and like my uncle said, it's worth a try.

I remember when my uncle started being kind to people. It felt weird because he wasn't that type of guy. The community didn't know him like that. He spent his whole life being locked up. And it hurt because that was time we lost. He wasn't bad; he just made bad decisions. But he also made me who I am, and I am proud of it. He taught me lots of things, like how to be respectful, caring, helpful, and kind to others. He was a great man. God let me borrow him for some years, and I am really thankful for that. I know that before he died, he wanted me to help change the world by being kind. Now I'm doing it in his memory.

Elia was born in 1999 in El Salvador. She moved to San Francisco during elementary school, and wrote this essay in 2015 with the help of an 826 Valencia tutor as part of the Young Authors' Book Project at Mission High School. In this project, students wrote essays about what they believe and why, published as the collection If The World Only Knew.

WHAT DO I REMEMBER ABOUT BEING 15?

now at 30

THESE DAYS NOT A WHOLE LOT

still dyed →

MOSTLY USELESS STUFF

Hair dyed red →
(oh that, middle part)

LIKE CLASS SCHEDULES
(spanish, bio, fashion design, english,
history, math, gym, art history, art)

OR LOCKER COMBOS
(0-30-8)

Some band shirt ←

→ necktie for a belt

pink parachute pants
(UFOs)

OR WHAT I WORE

teal Pumas

AND I REMEMBER FEELING INTENSELY DRAMATIC

then at 15

WHETHER FOR GOOD REASONS

The New York

<1 month
before 15

XX

OR (EVENTUALLY) SILLY ONES

wardrobe
malfunctions

BRACES

heartache

crying in
public

falling up
stairs

tripping
on a flat
surface

falling
down the
stairs

Drama

THE BEST THING YOU CAN DO IS LEARN HOW TO LAUGH

LAUGH AT YOUR DRAMA, LAUGH AT THE WORLD & ESPECIALLY LAUGH AT YOURSELF

YOU MIGHT TRIP LESS IF YOU STOP WITH THE BAGGY PANTS

WELL, SKINNY JEANS ARE TERRIBLE

ONE DAY YOU MIGHT NOT EVEN REMEMBER WHAT IT WAS ALL ABOU

Partial Recall

KAZ PALLADINO

This prompt was surprisingly difficult. It turned out my personal memories of being fifteen were slim and mostly overshadowed by what is arguably the most important event of 2001. Besides this, my general recollection of teenage years is not overtly fond or adoring (though take heart, I have been inclined toward cynicism). My reaction is to displace discomfort with humor, and though this might not be the best advice (before you psychoanalyze), humor has always helped me through the rough patches. The point of this piece was not to downplay the teenage experience, but to suggest taking a step out of the serious and intense moments (thanks hormones), and learn to keep light. The memories will be unreliable after all.

Kaz Palladino is a digital illustrator and owner of the brand Awkward Affections. She was born in New York and currently resides in San Francisco, where she received an MFA from Academy of Art University. Through her bright and quirky illustrations, she likes to explore the humor and universality of the human experience. You can view her work at awkwardaffections.com.

Longtime Correspondents

HANNAH KINGSLEY-MA

At fifteen I think I'm as smart, if not SMARTER, than most adults I know. I interpret fashion as wearing many different types of shirts on top of each other. That's how I go about my day, swaddled in three shirts artfully arranged. I spend a lot of time in front of my computer screen typing staccato messages to my friends from my AIM screen name "koalaelbow," which I've chosen only because "iguanabutt" was already taken.

Sometimes I'm so tired in the evening that I fall asleep on top of all my covers with an uncapped pen gripped in my hand. When I wake up there are puddles of blue ink blotted onto my blanket like the world's weirdest period stain. I am always late to school because I never wake up on time.

My high school is populated by fifteen-year-olds who are very prompt. It is a school that celebrates Rigor. It is a school that celebrates Winners. I do not relate to this. But I make it through because I have a secret that the other kids don't know: I want to be a writer. I've known this since I was very little. My mother picked up on this and enrolled me in a series of creative writing workshops at 826. It was there that I got to interact with Real Life Writers, who gave me prompts and carefully read my work. I was so greedy for those prompts! In those evenings I felt like I could see myself clearly. Like getting prescription sunglasses or wiping the fog off a mirror after too long and too hot of a shower.

But at fifteen I stop going to these workshops. That's because I am very focused on being a diligent yet forgettable student. As a result, writing becomes a secret pastime, likes eavesdropping or passing notes. I do not interact with Real Life Writers anymore.

Instead I spend my evenings running around the woods with the school's cross-country team. We are a smelly bunch. The striving is what makes us smelly. Every now and then a teacher will throw me a bone and allow creative writing assignments. We read Greek tragedies in my English class and I attempt to write my own. It's loosely based on John Edwards's fall from grace—the Democratic primaries are in full swing and I'm desperate to be considered "precocious." The play is very bad. It's told from the perspective of a betrayed wife who says things like "How *could* you do this to me, after all that we've *been through?*" I have a grand time writing it. I congratulate myself on a job well done, and think it up there in the pantheon of things Written by Adults. I write a short story about my best friend and next-door neighbor growing up, specifically my relationship to her two cats who have the same exact name. It's more or less entirely true but I tell everyone who reads it that it's a Fictionalized Account. *See?* I tell myself. *I'm already getting the hang of it.*

All this is to say that even though I write very little at age fifteen, and what I do write is frequently terrible, I never doubt the idea that one day it will be the very cornerstone of my life—how I will make all my future loads of money, and how people will come to regard me. At fifteen I don't feel too worried about how I'm going to make this all happen. Instead I sprint in literal circles, dreaming up what this life might look and feel like to my enlightened-adult self.

Now I'm no longer fifteen but twenty-six, and there are lots of predictable unknowns. The one that looms largest is that I have no idea whether I'll end up ever being a Real Life Writer. At times that makes me feel at odds with the fifteen-year-old me. Because even though she wrote strange and cloying things and never brushed her hair, she had an aura of certainty about her that I envy. She was so sure of what her future life would look like, of what it was she liked, of what it was she thought she was good at. I want to honor her monomaniac aspirations but I also want to be sensible, in the way adults should. So I try my hardest to not disappoint her, all the while making peace with the idea that I very well might. I still write in my diary in the dead of night and try and pay attention to the world in order to do so and run those same worn trails always always always leading to the ocean. Smelly from the striving. Me and her and her and I, longtime correspondents. We have more in common than we might like to think.

Hannah Kingsley-Ma is a radio producer, writer, and bookseller living in her hometown of San Francisco. Her work has appeared on KALW Public Radio, the CBC's Love Me, *KCRW and NPR's* Latino USA, *as well as* Literary Hub *and the* Rumpus. *As a middle schooler she attended 826 workshops, and she has since worked as a volunteer tutor, intern, workshop instructor, and Pirate Store employee.*

It's a Superpower

KEVIN G.

AGE 15 · MISSION HIGH SCHOOL

When I was in the first grade, my teacher told me that I had ADHD. I thought it was homework. I was sitting in class as Mr. M walked toward me. I was able to smell the pancakes he was making in the back of the class. The pancakes smelled like smooth butter and very nice, warm dough. In a somewhat sad voice, he told me that I had a condition. He said my condition meant that I couldn't sit still or concentrate as easily as others. He also told me that I was not able to sit still for a pretty long time. All of the students in my class heard Mr. M and started laughing. Then he told the students to stop yelling or he would not give us pancakes. And little tiny me was wanting to be cool so I yelled, "Yeah, what he said!" After all that, he told me it was called ADHD. The students didn't know what ADHD was, and I didn't either. The kids stopped playing with me and called me a bunch of mean and rude names.

One week later, I was lying on my white comfy couch thinking about what Mr. M told me in class. I told my mother about the disorder the teacher told me. And she explained to me that it was just a thing that makes it hard to sit still and concentrate. I was confused about the way this felt. Then she told me, "ADHD is not a disorder, it's a superpower."

I went to school the next day and explained what ADHD was to my classmates. They didn't care and started laughing more, so I told the teacher, and he explained it to my classmates. The kids in my class felt ashamed and wanted to be my friend. I said no because I didn't like them, and I just continued with my life. I was thinking that I didn't need rude and mean people in my life. I was also thinking about what my mom would be making for dinner when I got home.

A couple days later, I was playing at my school using the monkey bars. I was swinging toward the middle bar. While I was reaching the bar, I touched it and my hand slipped. I fell on the ground and landed on my back. While I was on the ground I started thinking about what my mom had said about ADHD while the pain was going away. I thought that I would be in a lot of pain, but I wasn't. I got right back up, and I really felt like ADHD was a superpower. When I got up and saw the teachers run toward me, I was standing proudly. And then, when the teachers saw me get up and run back toward the monkey bars, they were surprised like I was. Maybe they thought that I was a superhero, which is what I thought.

A time when I put this belief in action was about two or three months before I started high school. At my middle school over the summer, there was a skateboarding competition. It was statewide. I have never seen so many people sign up for a competition. It was the third round and there were five rounds in total. My brother was in the first, my friend Chris was in the second, and I was in the third. I was surprised that my brother was in first place for two rounds. My turn was sneaking up on me and I was trying to fight it off. I started to think negatively about falling or messing up on a trick. But then my mind flew away and I remembered what my mom told me in the first grade. Then I was ready. As the DJ was yelling my name, I was able to hear all the people in the crowds cheering for me. That made me happy. As I rolled out, I was pumped up as I was going up for my first trick, a five-stair kickflip, and I landed it with ease.

I think that it is not cool that there are no songs or movies that talk about ADHD. I think that Michael Bay needs to make a Transformers movie and make a car have ADHD. That would be cool. Another question is, why would there ever be a movie about ADHD? I think that most people think that ADHD is not anything important and think that it's a little cough or a small flu. But people get ADHD for life; it's not a little two- or three-day thing. It's forever. And sometimes it can mess people up very bad.

Now I know that I am not the only one with ADHD, and I was right—it is a superpower. This sends a message to other people: Just because I have a disorder does not make me any different from any other person. I am still the same person inside and out. Now I am in the ninth grade at Mission High School. I have not changed at all, not one bit. I am awesome, I can bake, cook, and skateboard. I am on the school baseball team. I love to play video games like there's no tomorrow. ADHD is attention deficit hyperactivity disorder. And just because I have this thing does not make me any different from anyone else.

Kevin was born in Honduras, and when he wrote this essay in 2015 he described himself as someone who "has swag, has a dog named Mia, and may or may not have a sixth toe." He wrote this essay with the help of an 826 Valencia tutor as part of the Young Authors' Book Project at Mission High School. In this project, 66 ninth graders wrote essays about what they believe and why, published as the collection If The World Only Knew.

Untitled

GABRIELLE H.

AGE 15 · JUNE JORDAN SCHOOL FOR EQUITY

LARS: geeky fifteen-year-old guy who has a huge ego
DEAN: shy fifteen-year-old football player
JEAN: sixteen-year-old cheerleader

Lars and Dean are sitting at the cafeteria table. Lars is halfway off his seat, trying to ask out girls who pass by their table.

LARS: HEY! HEY Melissa, wanna go out Saturday?! NO? Okay then, your loss. Hey Vivien, listen babe, I know you like me. . . so how about I take you out on Saturday, eh? [*Vivien gives him the finger*] I LOVE YOU TOO, BABE!

DEAN: DUDE WILL YOU SHUT UP ALREADY?! Dang, you're embarrassing yourself.

LARS: Pshhhh. . . Nah bro. . . I'm giving these girls the chance to go out with me. They're just shy.

DEAN: Shy? Really?

LARS: Yep. They're shy like how butterflies are when they first get their wings. . . Hey NICOLE! OVER HERE! [*waves*] WANNA GO OUT?!

DEAN: [*shakes his head*] You are desperate.

LARS: Am not. I'm just working my magic on these girls.

IN THE HALLWAY

Jean walks by.

JEAN: Hi Dean.

Dean stares at her but doesn't answer.

THAT AFTERNOON

LARS: Dude, no offense, but you don't know how to flirt.

DEAN: EXCUSE ME?!

LARS: Hey, hey, hey—I'm telling you this because I'm your friend, and I care about you. Now please put down my science fair project. I didn't work on it all night so you could break it because I insulted your man pride.

DEAN: For your information, mister, I know stuff, okay? I know stuff. I know girls.

LARS: [*smirks*] Oh really? All right, then. Prove it. Ask me out. I'll pretend to be Jean.

DEAN: P-pr-prove it? What do I even talk about?

LARS: Anything. The weather, the day. Mondays.

DEAN: Mondays?

LARS: Everyone hates Mondays.

LATER

Jean is by her locker. Dean approaches her in a feeble attempt to ask her out.

DEAN: Uh. . . hey Jean! [*his voice squeaks so he clears his throat*]

JEAN: Hi Dean, what's up?

DEAN: Nothin' [*high pitched*] much. [*clears throat*] How. . . how about you?

JEAN: Same old. . .

DEAN: SO. . . uh, cool. . . uh. . . Mondays. Whew. I hate Mondays. Don't you?

RANDOM PERSON WALKING BY: TGIF!

AFTER SCHOOL

LARS: Dude, how did you screw that up? C'mon, practice on me, ask me out.

DEAN: FINE! Hey, uh, hi Jean!

LARS: [*in a high pitched voice*] Oh hi Dean! What are you doing here in the girls' bathroom? You know you aren't allowed in here. . . Oh my gosh! Are you following me?!

DEAN: What the heck, Lars?! The girls' bathroom?! Are you freakin' serious?!

LARS: STAY IN CHARACTER, FOR CHRIST'S SAKE!

DEAN: No, I will not stay in character, because my character is stalking Jean in the girls' bathroom!

LARS: Can we just please please please pretty pretty please do this scene?

DEAN: Fine.

LARS: All right. Let's try it again. 3. . . 2. . . 1. . . ACTION!

DEAN: Hey Jean. . . I was just. . . just. . . w-w-wondering if you. . . uh. . . like. . . I mean. . . Do-you-have-a-pencil-I-could-borrow? [*Dean yelps in pain as Lars hit his head with a textbook*] What the hell, Lars?!

LARS: Are you freaking kidding me? A pencil?! A freaking pencil?! Do you have any idea how creepy that sounded?! Following her in to the girls' bathroom for a FREAKING PENCIL?! A FREAKING PENCIL?!

DEAN: Why are we in the bathroom in the first place? You're the one who made up this stupid scene! You're the one who made all of this creepy!

THE NEXT DAY

LARS: I am telling you, man, the best way to ask out a girl is by waiting for her after class.

DEAN: Seriously?

LARS: What's her last class?

DEAN: Well, first period she has honors bio with Rizzo. Second period she has English with Valdez. She has third with Goldstein for APUSH. Four is honors chem with Jones. Then honors study hall. Then sixth-period French with Toad, before cheer out on the field. Well, she walks to the locker room. So French, then locker room, then cheer.

LARS: Perfect. Meet her after French! PERFECT. Walk with her friends to the locker room.

DEAN: To the locker room?

LARS: You know where she'll be, and you know where she's going. This is perfect.

DEAN: The Monday idea was stupid, though.

LARS: This, my friend, is a great idea. Think positive. Dream big.

DEAN: Why would I be by the French classroom?

LARS: Just try it. Play it cool, man. Pretend you're picking up something or you got lost or something. I swear on my grandmother's grave you will get a date.

AFTER SIXTH PERIOD

Dean waits outside the classroom. The bell goes off, signaling that sixth period has ended.

JEAN: Oh, hi Dean!

DEAN: OH, HAHAHA, I didn't see you there. That's fine. . . sooo, uh, where are ya headed? Can I walk you there?

JEAN: Uh. . . the girls' locker room. . . yeah. . . I'm kinda waiting for my friends. . .

DEAN: Yeah. Well, I think I left my football. Around here.

JEAN: Here?

DEAN: I got lost.

JEAN: Okay, well. . . it's the girls' locker room.

DEAN: Oh okay. . . uh, I'll walk you to your friends, then?

JEAN: No, I got this. Thank you, though.

DEAN: Uh. . . [*shakes her hand*] Bye!

THAT AFTERNOON

They are on the field. The cheerleaders are practicing nearby. Lars and Dean toss a football.

LARS: Oh, so now it's my fault?! All I did was try and help you, but you BLEW IT! CUZ YOU SUCK!

DEAN: God forbid I catch you, because I will break every single bone in your body!

LARS: GET AWAY FROM ME!

Lars and Dean start tackling each other. We hear a cheer: two, four, six, eight. . .

LARS: Look at them angels fly. Such beauty. Look at their blond hair bounce. . . Their skirts bounce with the wind like rose petals. [*ad lib exaggerated commentary*]

Dean looks at Lars. Dean walks toward Jean and hands her the football.

JEAN: Oh hi, Dean. What's up?

DEAN: Can I ask you a question?

JEAN: Sure.

DEAN: Would you go on a date with me?

JEAN: Oh? Okay!

Dean looks back to Lars. A "How you like these apples?" gesture. Jean gives him a basketball.

SATURDAY

Saturday. Seven o'clock. Dean is with Jean in a diner eating.

DEAN: You look. . . really pretty. . .

Jean is eating spaghetti.

JEAN: Thanks.

DEAN: So. . . uh. . .

Awkward silence.

JEAN: What?

DEAN: Nothing.

Dean smiles. Jean smiles.

THE END

Gabby wrote this play during the 2015 Young Authors' Workshop at 826 Valencia, and it was first published in the chapbook Each Blaring Hue. *It was later performed at her school. Gabby went on to join the Youth Leadership Advisory Board at 826 Valencia, serving as a mentor and tutor in our programs.*

How to Become a Writer

JACQUELINE M.

AGE 17 · SAN MATEO HIGH SCHOOL

Have you ever looked yourself in the mirror on a calm afternoon and thought to yourself, *Gee, I wonder what it's like to write a book. . . ?* Probably not, but let's pretend that you have, to avoid an awkward situation.

Well, look nor question any further, because this book that is presented to you is no ordinary book, but a guide to becoming a successful writer!* By following these easy steps, you'll be scribbling down stories like a pro.

First, get inspired! Try watching that one movie your friend has been begging you to watch about the two random girls that turn into cars. After all, you might get an idea and a chuckle out of it. If you're feeling nostalgic, look back on your favorite book or TV series and loosely focus on an element that you loved the most, like the concept or setting. Just don't plagiarize anything unless you want a rabid author chasing after you in an attempt to sue you.

Second step: Come up with a basic, general idea. What kind of genre do you want to tackle? Horror? Fantasy? Slice of life? Basic plot? Characters? Don't worry about the exact details yet. We'll come back to it later.

Number three, come up with characters. Maybe base them off of real people, or go wild! Just don't make them generic, sparkly vampires when you can do so much better than that. Perhaps a vampire that hates drinking blood and instead tries to live off of

---

* Remember, the Bass Corporation is not responsible for any mishaps you get involved in, such as lawsuits; additionally, it is not our fault if you feel that this guide is null and useless. So too bad, so sad, you're stuck with this manual!

caffeine while dealing with an exhausting office job. Sounds weird? Good.

Step four is also known as the dreaded step of doom. This step will make you cry and scream like a newborn baby: writing the darn plot. I can't really help you with this, since, well, I kinda suck at it. Just go Google it or something.

Here comes step five: making your characters suffer! I'm pretty sure 90 percent of the plot should rely on your characters crawling into a ball and sobbing. Where does the other 10 percent go? Well, that's your own choice! Anyway, your main character has a little sister? Aw, how cute. Break her and her optimism, but not too much. After all, she needs to develop as a character. You can't get carried away with the gut-wrenching backstory with your brooding main character deciding to get revenge on the villain for stealing the last cookie! They need to grow and blossom as a person in order for the readers to be able to relate and empathize with them.

Plus, it's decent payback against your writing buddies who have repeatedly dragged their characters into the void of despair, aiming to irritate you. Just avoid social media when you publish your book since there's probably going to be a mob of vicious fans online harshly condemning you for making little Becky cry. But, hey, it was totally worth it, right?

Now, after five taxing steps, it's time to draft out your story.

"But, wait, Jacqueline!" you adamantly howl, desperate to argue with me. "I don't have any good ideas!"

Well, you know what, Johnny? You're just as wrong as the idea of leaving eggs on your sidewalk on a blistering and savage August day. Everyone has potential! Yes, even lazy Jimmy in the corner of the room, who constantly complains about literature and despises it with a burning, scorching-hot passion. No matter what, you should try new things despite the possible end results or others' opinions.

Now it is time for step is—what's this? You finished drafting your story? Congratulations! It's time for you to introduce your story to your fellow writers!

Huh? You're experiencing the notorious IATOSMW (pronounced *eye-ought-smw*. . . or something like that) sickness that, according to some random statistic found on Google, prevents millions of writers from sharing their stories each year? You haven't heard of this? Well, time to give a brief history lesson on this infamous illness. First things first: What does IATOSMW stand for? That's easy. It stands for:

I

Am

Terrified

Of

Sharing

My

Work

Symptoms of IATOSMW include sweaty palms, procrastination, butterflies in your stomach, mumbling, and passionately hoping that you won't get chosen to read your story out loud. On the other hand, how do you cure this ailment?

Well. . . you can't. A magical fairy isn't going to spontaneously poof into existence when they hear your cry for help and wave a silver, glistening wand to banish your fear of public speaking. It takes an abundance of time to overcome stage fright, and if you try to avoid sharing your work, it can worsen over time (you don't want to end up like me, folks). All you can do is repeatedly share your work and patiently listen to others' feedback. After all, what's the worst that can happen? It's rather unlikely the person you are reading your story to will hurl your rough draft against the wall and shriek about how horrible and repulsive your work is, right?

From here on out, you're on your own, kid. What awaits you now is the puzzling road to publishing your story that is filled with obstacles and uncertainty. However, do not fret, since you have people on your side to support and cheer you on! It may take long, grueling years for your story to break free from the rough draft stage and be published, but you'll get there. Somehow.

Jacqueline wrote this piece in the fall of 2016 in the Writing and Publishing Apprentices workshop at 826 Valencia. It was inspired to Lorrie Moore's short story "How To Be a Writer," and Jacqueline even overcame her own IATOSMW and read the piece for a packed house of friends and family at the end of the workshop! The piece was first publisehd in the chapbook Umbrellas and the Universe, *and in the 826* Quarterly, *vol. 25.*

With Love from 826 Day

THE 826 VALENCIA COMMUNITY

On August 26, 2017, we threw our own biggest birthday party ever and invited our whole community to join us for a block party to celebrate fifteen years of 826 Valencia. We asked our guests and passers-by to share a few words about being fifteen, or make lists of fifteen things. (Making lists is very satisfying.) We present to you here some of the words of wisdom friends and strangers shared on Valencia Street that day.

Fifteen Ways to Show Compassion

1. Cook food for others.

2. Hug for an extra second.

3. Sit and listen.

4. Watch other peoples' favorite TV shows with them, even if you don't like it.

5. Create art! For other people!

—**Hanna M.**

6. Smile.

7. Say good morning.

8. Give someone your seat on the bus.

9. Ask them how their day is going.

10. Give them some gum.

—**Rachel K.**

11. Get over yourself.

12. Lead.

13. Stick with projects.

14. Make eye contact.

15. Stay in touch.

—Nnamdi F.

Advice For Your Fifteen-Year-Old Self, in Fifteen Words

Don't straighten your hair. There are lots of reasons for this. Just don't do it. —**Jessica S.**

Worried that real life will be just like high school? Prepare to be pleasantly surprised. —**Kevin W.**

Don't entertain your friends at someone else's expense. I've regretted it for decades, and counting. —**Thao N.**

Remind yourself daily: The real world's not scary, and high school is, thankfully, just temporary. —**Michelle R.**

Fifteen People to Admire (at fifteen, or any age)

1. Maddie Banstein

2. Dylan Marron

3. Franchesca Ramscy

4. Julie Abraham

5. Sayuri Oyama

6. Kamala Harris

7. Jinkx Monsoon

8. Komozi Woodard

9. Kim Christensen

10. Nicki Minaj

11. Terry Pratchett

12. Maurice Sendak

13. Ursula K. LeGuin

14. James Baldwin

15. Me!

—Frances M.

ABOUT 826 VALENCIA

Who We Are

STAFF

Bita Nazarian *Executive Director*

Alyssa Aninag *Volunteer Coordinator*
Dana Belott *Programs Coordinator*
Elaina Bruna *Development Coordinator*
Lizzie Jean Coyle *Individual Philanthropy Officer*
Ricardo Cruz Chong *Programs Associate*
Shelby Dale DeWeese, *Programs Coordinator*
Lauren Hall *Grants and Evaluations Director*
Allyson Halpern *Development Director*
Caroline Kangas *Stores Manager*
Kona Lai *Programs Coordinator*
Kiley McLaughlin *Programs Coordinator*
Molly Parent *Communications and Programs Manager*
Christina V. Perry *Director of Education*
Amy Popovich *Production Manager*
Kathleen Rodriguez *Programs Manager*
Meghan Ryan *Design Director*
Ashley Smith *Programs Manager*
Anton Timms *Volunteer Engagement Director*
Jillian Wasick *Programs Manager*
Byron Weiss *Assistant Stores Manager*
Ryan Young *Programs Manager*

BOARD OF DIRECTORS

Eric Abrams	Michelle Yunhi Lee	Andrew Strickman
Colleen Quinn Amster	Alex Lerner	Joe Vasquez
Joya Banerjee	Jim Lesser	Rachel Swain Yeaman
Barb Bersche	Dave Pell	
Lisa Brown	Han Phung	

COFOUNDERS

Nínive Calegari and Dave Eggers

OUR VOLUNTEERS

There's absolutely no way we could create hundreds of publications and serve thousands of students annually without a legion of volunteers. These incredible people work in all realms, from tutoring to fundraising and beyond. They range in age, background, and expertise, but all have a shared passion for our work with young people. Volunteers past and present, you know who you are. Thank you, thank you, thank you.

826 NATIONAL

826 Valencia's success has spread across the country. Under the umbrella of 826 National, writing and tutoring centers have opened in six more cities. If you would like to learn more about other 826 programs, please visit the following websites.

826 National 826national.org	**826 DC** 826dc.org	**826 NYC** 826nyc.org
826 Boston 826boston.org	**826 LA** 826la.org	**826 Valencia** 826valencia.org
826 Chicago 826chi.org	**826 Michigan** 826michigan.org	

What We Do

826 Valencia is a San Francisco–based nonprofit organization dedicated to supporting under-resourced students ages six to eighteen with their writing skills, and to helping teachers get their students excited about writing. Our work is based on the understanding that great leaps in learning can be made when trained and caring volunteers work one-on-one with students and that strong writing skills are fundamental to future success.

826 Valencia comprises two writing centers—our flagship location in the Mission district and a new center in the Tenderloin neighborhood—and three satellite classrooms at nearby schools. Both of our centers are fronted by kid-friendly, weird, and whimsical stores, which serve as portals to learning and gateways for the community. All of our programs are offered free of charge. Since we first opened our doors in 2002, thousands of volunteers have dedicated their time to working with tens of thousands of students.

OUR PROGRAMS

FIELD TRIPS

Classes from public schools around San Francisco visit our writing centers for a morning of high-energy learning about the craft of storytelling. Four days a week, our Field Trips produce bound, illustrated books and professional-quality podcasts, infusing creativity, collaboration, and the arts into students' regular school day.

IN-SCHOOLS PROGRAMS

We bring teams of volunteers into high-need schools around the city to support teachers and provide one-on-one assistance to students as they tackle various writing projects, including newspapers, research papers, oral histories, and more. We have a special presence at Buena

Vista Horace Mann K–8, Everett Middle School, and Mission High School, where we staff dedicated Writers' Rooms throughout the school year.

AFTER-SCHOOL TUTORING

During the school year, 826 Valencia's centers are packed five days a week with neighborhood students who come in after school, in the evenings, and on Sundays for tutoring in all subject areas, with a special emphasis on creative writing and publishing. During the summer, these students participate in our five-week Exploring Words Summer Camp, where we explore science and writing through projects, outings, and activities in a super-fun educational environment.

WORKSHOPS

826 Valencia offers workshops designed to foster creativity and strengthen writing skills in a wide variety of areas, from playwriting to personal essays to starting a zine. All workshops, from the playful to the practical, are project-based and are taught by experienced, accomplished professionals. Over the summer, our Young Authors' Workshop provides a two-week intensive writing experience for high-school-age students.

COLLEGE AND CAREER READINESS

We offer a roster of programs designed to help students get into college and be successful there. Every year we provide six $15,000 scholarships to college-bound seniors and provide one-on-one support to 200 students via the Great San Francisco Personal Statement Weekend. We also offer internships, peer tutoring stipends, and career workshops to our youth leaders.

PUBLISHING

Students in all of 826 Valencia's programs have the opportunity to explore, experience, and celebrate themselves as writers in part because of our professional-quality publishing. In addition to the book you're holding, 826 Valencia publishes newspapers, magazines, chapbooks, podcasts, and blogs—all written by students.

TEACHER OF THE MONTH

From the beginning, 826 Valencia's goal has been to support teachers. We aim to both provide the classroom support that helps our hardworking teachers meet the needs of all our students and to celebrate their important work. Every month, we receive letters from students, parents, and educators nominating outstanding teachers for our Teacher of the Month award, which comes with a $1,500 honorarium. Know an SFUSD teacher you want to nominate? Guidelines can be found at 826valencia.org.

VISIT US!

You can visit 826 Valencia, peruse our student-written publications, stock up on supplies for the working buccaneer or world adventurer, and interact with the wonders within. Sometimes the wonders will even interact with you.

What are we talking about? Come visit our stores!

THE PIRATE SUPPLY STORE

826 Valencia Street
San Francisco, CA 94110
Daily, 12:00 – 6:00 p.m.

KING CARL'S EMPORIUM

180 Golden Gate Avenue
San Francisco, CA 94102
Monday – Friday, 11:00 a.m.– 5:00 p.m.

SHOP ONLINE

826valencia.org/store

Other Books from 826 Valencia

826 Valencia produces a variety of publications, each of which contains work written by students in our various programs. Some are professionally printed and nationally distributed; others are glued together here and sold in our stores. These projects represent some of the most exciting work at 826 Valencia, as they enable Bay Area students to experience a world of publishing not otherwise available to them. Visit *826valencia.org/store* or your local bookstore to purchase the following publications:

We Are Here, Walking Toward the Unknown (**2017**) Have you been misunderstood or judged? What fears are you working to overcome? Can science and technology go too far? If you had the opportunity to go back, how would you fix a past mistake? While these questions were inspired by the themes in Mary Shelley's *Frankenstein*, a book written in the nineteenth century, they are still as thought-provoking and relevant as ever. In this collection, the seniors of Burton High School in San Francisco set out to answer them in the form of personal narratives, fictional short stories, and letters. From intimate reflections about their own lived experiences to the development of creative and futuristic worlds, these young authors meditate on our past, present, and future.

Walk the Earth in Our Shoes and Plant Some Seeds Behind You (**2016**) collects personal essays from students at John O'Connell High School. What would we learn if we could interview a whale? Is diversity as advantageous in a social community as it is in a coral reef? How does our environment affect us, and how do we affect our environment? These questions are both age-old and urgent, and in this collection, ninth- and tenth-grade authors set out to answer them. From how their neighborhoods are changing to what it's like to live in a drought, these young authors share their views and experiences as they investigate the way ecosystems work—and their answers hold insights everyone should read.

If the World Only Knew (2015) is a collection of essays written by sixty-six freshmen at Mission High School. In this book students reflect on their beliefs and where they come from—the people who influenced them, the times when they were most necessary, and the ways in which the world has tested them. The collection is a testament to the power of personal conviction, and a powerful case for why young people's voices should be heard—and believed.

Uncharted Places (2014) is a collection of essays by fifty-two juniors and seniors at Thurgood Marshall High School that examines the idea of "place" and what it means to these young authors. It contains stories about locales real and imagined, internal and external, places of transition and those of comfort. These young writers bravely share their views of the world, giving us a glimpse into the places that are most important to them—those not necessarily found on a map, but in the heart.

The Enter Question (2013) is a collection of essays on issues of immigrant identity recounted in eighty-one distinct voices from the eleventh-grade class at San Francisco International High School. The collection covers a wide variety of topics including the challenges of communicating in a new language, the courage it takes to ask for help, and the joy found in meeting new people from all over the world, in addition to challenges all teenagers face as they struggle to forge identity and community. *(Out of print)*

Arrive, Breathe, and Be Still (2012) is a collection of monologues and plays exploring the themes of resistance and resilience written by thirty-five students at Downtown High School in San Francisco, with a foreword by playwright Octavio Solis. After a semester of working intensely with actors at the American Conservatory Theater and writing tutors from 826 Valencia, the students produced this powerful look into the realities of high school life, the pressures surrounding young people, and the strength it takes to keep going. Perfect for reading or performing, these pieces are a refreshing tool for using theater both in the classroom and outside of it.

Beyond Stolen Flames, Forbidden Fruit, and Telephone Booths (2011) is a collection of essays and short stories, written by fifty-three juniors and seniors at June Jordan School for Equity, in which young writers explore the role of myth in our world today. Students wrote pieces of fiction and nonfiction, retelling old myths, creating new ones, celebrating everyday heroes, and recognizing the tales that their families have told over and over. With a foreword by Khaled Hosseini, the result is a collection with a powerful message about the stories that have shaped students' perspectives and the world they know.

A Time to Eat Cake (2011) is a collection of short pieces from the students in 826 Valencia's After-School Tutoring program. In collaboration with the San Francisco pastry shop Miette, students spent a month exploring memories, imagining their ideal treats, and spinning amazing tales of cake adventures. With a foreword by Miette founder Meg Ray, this book shows that you don't have to be Proust to know the power of sweets. *(Out of print)*

We the Dreamers (2010) is a collection of essays by fifty-one juniors at John O'Connell High School reflecting on what the American dream means to them. The students recount stories about family, home, immigration, hardship, and the hopes of their generation—as well as those of the generation that raised them. The result is a firsthand account of these essayists' often-complicated relationship with our national ethos that is insightful, impassioned, surprising, and of utmost importance to our understanding of what the American dream means for their generation. *(Out of print)*

Show of Hands (2009) is a collection of stories and essays written by fifty-four juniors and seniors at Mission High School. It amplifies the students' voices as they reflect on one of humanity's most revered guides for moral behavior: the Golden Rule, which tells us that we should act toward others as we would want them to act toward us. Whether speaking about global issues, street violence, or the way to behave among friends and family, the voices of these young essayists are brilliant, thoughtful, and, most of all, urgent.

Thanks, and Have Fun Running the Country (**2009**) is a collection of letters penned by our After-School Tutoring students to newly elected President Obama. In this collection, which arrived at inauguration time, there's loads of advice for the president, often hilarious, sometimes heartfelt, and occasionally downright practical. The letters have been featured in the *New York Times* and the *San Francisco Chronicle*, and on *This American Life*.

I Live Real Close to Where You Used to Live (**2010**) is a collection of letters to Michelle, Sasha, Malia, and Bo Obama written by students across the 826 network. These letters are packed with questions, advice, and the occasional request to be invited over to the White House for dinner.

Seeing Through the Fog (**2008**) is a guidebook written by seniors from Gateway High School that explores San Francisco from tourist, local, and personal perspectives. Both whimsical and factually accurate, the pieces in this collection take the reader to the places that teenagers know best, from taquerias to skate spots to fashionable shops that won't break your budget. *(Out of print)*

Exactly (**2007**) is a hardbound book of colorful stories for children ages nine to eleven. This collection of fifty-six narratives by students at Raoul Wallenberg Traditional High School is illustrated by forty-three professional artists. It passes on lessons that teenagers want the next generation to know.

Inspired by magical realism, students at Galileo Academy of Science and Technology produced ***Home Wasn't Built in a Day*** (**2006**), a collection of short stories based on family myths and legends. With a foreword by actor and comedian Robin Williams, the book comes alive through powerful student voices that explore just what it is that makes a house a home.

I Might Get Somewhere: Oral Histories of Immigration and Migration (**2005**) exhibits an array of student-recorded oral narratives about moving to San Francisco both from other parts of the country and the world. Acclaimed author Amy Tan wrote the foreword to this compelling collection of personal stories by Balboa High

School students. These narratives shed light on the problems and pleasures of finding one's life in new surroundings. *(Out of print)*

Written by thirty-nine students at Thurgood Marshall Academic High School, **Waiting to Be Heard: Youth Speak Out About Inheriting a Violent World** (**2004**) addresses violence and peace on a personal, local, and global scale. With a foreword by Isabel Allende, the essays, fiction, poetry, and experimental writing create a passionate collection of student expression. *(Out of print)*

Talking Back: What Students Know About Teaching (**2003**) is a book that delivers the voices of the class of 2004 from Leadership High School. In reading the book—previously a required-reading textbook at San Francisco State University and Mills College—you will understand the relationships students want with their teachers, how students view classroom life, and how the world affects them. *(Out of print)*

PUBLICATIONS FOR STUDENTS & TEACHERS

Don't Forget to Write (**2005**) contains fifty-four of the best lesson plans used in workshops taught at 826 Valencia, 826NYC, and 826LA, giving away all of our secrets for making writing fun. Each lesson plan was written by its original workshop teacher, including Jonathan Ames, Aimee Bender, Dave Eggers, Erika Lopez, Julie Orringer, Jon Scieszka, Sarah Vowell, and many others. If you are a parent or a teacher, this book is meant to make your life easier, as it contains enthralling and effective ideas to get your students writing. It can also be used as a resource for the aspiring writer. In 2011, 826 National published a two-volume second edition of *Don't Forget to Write,* also available in our stores.

STEM to Story (**2015**) contains dynamic lesson plans that use hands-on discovery and creative writing to teach students about science, technology, engineering, and math. These quirky exploratory lessons are sure to awaken the imagination and ignite passions for both STEM and creative writing. *STEM to Story* is a boon to teachers, parents, and students alike, as each lesson plan is aligned with Common Core and Next Gen Science Standards.

It's Always a Good Time to Give

WE NEED YOUR HELP

We could not do this work without the thousands of volunteers who make our programs possible. We are always seeking more volunteer tutors, and volunteers with design, illustration, and photography skills. It's easy to become a volunteer and a bunch of fun to actually do it.

Please fill out our online application to let us know how you'd like to lend your time:

826valencia.org/get-involved/volunteer

OTHER WAYS TO GIVE

Whether it's loose change or heaps of cash, a donation of any size will help 826 Valencia continue to offer a variety of free writing and publishing programs to Bay Area youth.

Please make a donation at:
826valencia.org/donate

You can also mail your contribution to:
826 Valencia Street, San Francisco, CA 94110
Your donation is tax-deductible. What a plus! Thank you!

The 826 Actually-Quarterly Subscription

The 826 Actually-Quarterly Subscription
delivers brilliant student writing to your doorstep
four times a year.

4 TIMES A YEAR!

[unlike the 826 Quarterly, which comes out twice a year]

FOR ONLY $75, YOU'LL RECEIVE:

The Spring Quarterly

Filled with the best student writing from the semester.

Our latest Young Authors' Book Project

The Fall Quarterly

A Surprise Gift

Including some wisdom and whimsy
from our students and our store.

TO SUBSCRIBE, PLEASE VISIT:

826valencia.org/subscribe